# boyce...Boyce

## *A Memoir*

**Boyce L. Young**

boyce…Boyce

Copyright @ 2024 by Boyce L. Young

All rights reserved.

ISBN: 9798355185879

Published in the United States.

*This book is dedicated to my family.*

# boyce...Boyce

## *A Memoir*

### Boyce L. Young

# FOREWORD
# BY BOYCE L. YOUNG

*"boyce...Boyce"* is not intended to be a definitive work of precisely detailed history. (This book is nothing more than the author's best shot at being honest (by his memory) and a few details that he was able to obtain from numerous sources, some reliable and some maybe not so reliable.)

This book is intended to provide at least some of the details of my life for the enjoyment of my children, grandchildren, great-grandchildren, and future generations. It is not my intent to defame or dishonor any individual or individuals. If this occurs, please be aware that it is unintentional, and to any such individual, you have my deepest apologies. These are my recollections, and I have been accurate and honest to the best of my ability and memory.

This should be read with the understanding that it is from my unique perspective and "lenses" through which I perceive the experiences of my life. Others may see the same event with totally different outcomes. I intend to present my recalled history of many (not all) of my life's adventures as accurately as possible, with consummate integrity, authenticity, and respect for all family members and others.

My family, of the utmost importance to me, includes those who have passed on, those who are present in my life today, and those who will live and create my future descendants well after I've passed on.

Please note that this book is intended to be a partial genealogy record of the Young, Alexander, Goodin, Wells, and Franks family histories. It is only the beginning for those who are curious enough to proceed.

I hope other family members can use this book as a springboard for more extensive research into this extraordinary family. I know that I will continue my research and attempt to make that information available for family members and others as long as my God allows it. "That's my story, and I'm sticking to it!"

Yours, Boyce

# FOREWORD
# BY AVIS JOSEPHINE
# ALEXANDER HALL

I am the youngest of six siblings. My only brother, W.A., was eighteen and a half years old when I was born. Less than a year and a half after my birth World War II broke out, and my only brother joined the Army and went off to war. I never really knew my brother when I was a child. W.A. passed away when I was only twenty- six years old.

I have no childhood memories of my brother. When Boyce came to live with us, I was eleven, and he was around two years old, and I immediately took Boyce under my wing, and we were more like" big sister" and "little brother" than aunt and nephew.

I remember when Boyce started school. He boarded that big yellow school bus with tears rolling down his precious face. I had to get pretty stern with him and remind him that the kids would likely make fun of him, and they did. But I gave them a piece of my mind, which quickly ended!

I am so proud of all that Boyce has accomplished in his lifetime. When I read this memoir, I realized that he had experienced many things of which I wasn't even aware. Boyce has proven that you can overcome whatever comes your way if you choose to do so.

Boyce, you have made all of us proud.
I love you so much, "Little Brother!"

Your Sister and Aunt,
Avis Josephine Alexander Hall
Olive Branch, Mississippi, August 2022

# FOREWORD
# BY KIMBERLY JOANNA
# YOUNG PATTERSON

Boyce Young has held many titles in his lifetime (some of which you'll read about in this book). Those titles include son, father, brother, friend, husband, Marine, and more. And yet, my favorites are "Daddy," "Pops," and "PaPa." Daddy is the first man I ever loved and the first man who loved me. This man has been that larger-than-life figure to my brothers and me; decidedly, he is the best man we have ever known.

I remember giving Daddy a journal several years ago for Christmas and asking him to write down his life's memories as he thought of them. I knew he wouldn't be here to tell them one day, and I wanted them around forever. That leather journal probably still sits empty on the bookshelf in his study.

This book is that journal in its best form. It tells the stories of a boy who shaped the courage of a soldier, the Marine who adapted and overcame through sheer determination, and the life experiences that shaped the perseverance and integrity of the man he became.

It is personal and honest, and its pages testify to his love for his family. Whether reading this book as a family member or a friend, I am so glad that we can all know a little more about the man we love dearly. This memoir is something that I will truly treasure forever.

With everlasting love,
Kimberly J. (Young) Patterson,
Brunswick, Georgia, August 2022

# FOREWORD
# BY BOYCE L. YOUNG, JR.

To almost everyone I know, their father invokes a strong emotional response...some good, some not so good. I am one of the lucky ones. It has been one of the greatest honors of my life to share my father's name. Many people that know me and my family think my son is named after me. Although there is no real way to distinguish, he is proudly named after my dad.

This book is something I never thought I'd have the pleasure to see come to fruition. I always hoped that I would have something permanent in my hands to share with my children about my father, but I was never certain if or how that would manifest.

Even though I have never subscribed to a strong desire to know my family roots as far back as documentation can track, I have a deep interest in the one man who has meant more to me than all others. I have always been interested in what shaped him.

He is one of the most remarkable men I have ever known and has been the father I needed in every stage of life. Although no one is ever perfect, he gave me the mark to aim for as a dad. Outside of this father role, I knew there was an incredible life full of hardships, trials, disappointments, and triumphs, of which I knew very little.

This book allows everyone to get a glimpse of the man I am proud to call my dad, but more importantly, it gives our family a lasting reminder of a person we have always cherished…our Pops.

With love, Boyce L Young,, Jr.
Thunderbolt, GA,, January 2023

# FOREWORD
# BY BYRON CARLISS YOUNG

My dad's life story has always been a mystery to me. And yet, one that I knew would make a great story once written down. I was impressed by the reality of knowing him my whole life and getting to know him in a completely different way through these pages.

This book will appeal to his relatives and anyone who might think the average American life looks the same for all. I could not be prouder to say that this man has shaped the person I am today. I'm forever grateful for the hard work and love that he has shown our country and our family.

With love, Byron C. Young
Toccoa, GA, December 2022

# FOREWORD BY ALISON RENEE' HERRINGTON HAND

Boyce Young, Sr., is my stepfather. It is a very rare occasion that I refer to him as such. For the past 24 years, I have called him my "Para- Dad," and he calls me his "Para-Child." Honestly, I cannot recall why we decided upon these titles. I don't recall discussing what to call one another; it just happened. Like a biological child, I cannot remember when I didn't know Boyce. How is this possible? Let me tell you, dear readers, OUR story.

Boyce and my mom worked for the Thomas & Hutton Engineering Company in Savannah, GA (which I will refer to as "T&H"). When I was a young child, T&H was a small and very family- focused company. It was common for employees' children and spouses to stop in for a visit.

My mom was a single mom, and there were occasions when I was allowed to stay at T&H after school, before or after sports practices, etc. I would sit in the kitchen and do homework or some other activity to keep busy and quiet.

Employees intermittently came in for a quick break, and we chatted. One such employee was Boyce. He would come into the kitchen and talk to me for a bit. He was always friendly and kind, and I genuinely liked him. He tells me I was "a sassy little thing" back then, but I don't recall that!

Over the years, T&H had many events for employees and their families. Boyce and his family were always there, so, I grew up knowing Kimberly, Boyce Jr., and Byron. I had no idea they would one day be family.

Fast forward to December 5, 1998. My parents were married, and that was the day I officially lost the title of "only child." I became a Para-Daughter, sister, sister-in-law, and aunt. I tell the story above when people ask how my parents met, yet there is so much more.

I tell them sincerely that I could have NEVER hand-picked a better man to be my mom's husband and my dad. I have witnessed on countless occasions the fierce love he has for me, my mom, his children, and our extended family.

Has it always been sunshine and smiley faces? Of course not! As with all families, there are trying situations, disagreements, and growing pains... our family is no different. What I can tell you is that there is love.

As you will read, Boyce has yet to lead an easy life. I have often thought about how easy it would have been for him to be a victim of circumstances he had no control over. He could have taken any other life path, but he chose this one. He chose to join the Marines and fight for his country.

He chose to further his education and become a Professional Land Surveyor. He chose godliness instead of bitterness. He chose to be my dad instead of just the man who married my mom, and I am forever grateful. He decided to be this Boyce Young who is respected by so many and adored by me.

Love,

Your Para-Daughter who

"Loves You to the Moon,"

Alison R. Hand,

Yakima, Washington,

December 2022

# ACKNOWLEDGEMENTS

I want to thank my entire family, wife, children, aunts, cousins, nieces, nephews, etc. There are way too many to recognize individually, even though I'd like to be able to do so. Should I attempt to name them all, I'm sure I'd leave someone out, and I certainly don't want to do that. I'd like to first thank my wife of 24 years, Dianne, for tolerating me over the past couple of years. Even though she was experiencing a life-threatening health condition, she kept encouraging me to complete this book of memoirs of some of the most notable events in my life.

I'd also like to give a special thanks to my sweet Aunt Avis. In 2022, Avis lost her husband, Bobby, after sixty-four years of marriage. During her grief, she still took the time to gather a treasure trove of information, including photographs, names, dates, etc. She is and has always been my very sweet aunt.

I'd also like to thank my children for their encouragement in completing this work. This book would never have happened if it weren't for them, my grandchildren and great-grandchild. This book is for all my descendants.

Lastly, and yet, by no means least, I'd like to thank my editor, Pat Merritt. I met (Ms.) Pat several times at strategic planning retreats for the Development Authority of Bryan County (DABC), where she facilitated the meetings and discussions.

These retreats were comprised of a relatively small number of individuals, including the DABC staff, some Bryan County Commissioners, the county administrator, engineering representatives, and the DABC board of directors.

Every evening we always had a meal at a local restaurant and maybe drinks in the bar afterward. During one of these retreats on Saint Simons Island, Georgia, in November 2021, during the World Series when the Atlanta Braves won the world championship, Ms. Pat convinced me to follow my wife's and my children's wishes and capture some details of my life experiences.

She gracefully volunteered to edit the work and encouraged me to complete it. Without Ms. Pat's encouragement and steadfast giving of her time, all with extraordinary patience, this book would never have been possible. I will forever be grateful to Pat and her husband, Buz, for supporting her work with this poor, poorly educated boy from Mississippi.

Deep gratitude goes out to all who have participated in this book. The saying goes, "You can't take it with you." I believe that our family's stories of love, dedication, faith, and overcoming whatever is put in front of you are the most important assets of all.

If one isn't careful, they can easily carry life-long memories with them that would and should be treasured by descendants forever. One of the things that attempting to author this book has taught me is that everyone who is able should prepare and memorialize their memories for their families.

Boyce L. Young, Sr.
Black Creek, GA, December 2022

# EDITOR'S NOTES

As a trained strategic planning facilitator for the past 38 years, working on behalf of Georgia's 41 not-for- profit electric cooperatives, I have facilitated many county and regional development authority board retreats. The Development Authority of Bryan County (DABC) is a highly functioning development authority board. The DABC members who served on the board from 2016 to 2022 made great decisions in hiring professional staff and supporting them by making wise decisions requiring true and authentic servant leadership.

Over the past 7 years, I have gotten to know each of the DABC's board members, as there was a great deal of consistency on this board (another reason for its high level of function). Boyce Young of Black Creek, GA served for many years as the DABC's Secretary on the Executive Committee. During breaks in the board retreats and at group meals, I heard snippets of Boyce's life history. Remember, these retreats were conducted over only 1 and 1/2 days annually.

At every annual DABC board retreat, I would learn another fascinating fact about this man's experiences. He was always direct, honest, and pragmatic in delivering these facts. I would ask questions, and if he didn't feel comfortable answering them, he would say so, and I completely accepted his response.

In November 2021, at the annual DABC board retreat, I urged Boyce to turn his life experiences into a journal or memoir. He mentioned that his daughter, Kimberly, regularly encouraged him to do the same. I felt so strongly about preserving and sharing his experiences with his children, grandchildren, and great-grandchild that I offered to edit the journal for him. Granted, I am not a professionally trained book editor, so please do not judge this book by its editing.

The most important mission of this book is to capture the incredibly diverse and fascinating life of the man known as Boyce to some, Pops and Daddy to his kids, and PaPa to his grandchildren and great-grandchild. He is one of the most blessed men I know because he has survived and thrived through many hardships.

Boyce is incredibly resilient, talented, humble, and optimistic. His large, wonderfully loving family means everything in the world to him. As his editor, I encouraged Boyce to make notes of life experiences, send me photos from the family archives and keep writing regularly. I know that I got on his nerves many times. It has truly been a pleasure and an honor for me to help Boyce capture his memoirs for his beloved family in book form.

With greatest respect,
(Ms.) Pat B. Merritt
Smoke Rise, GA, October 2022

# THE BEGINNING OF MY STORY

## Boyce Leslie Young
## born on 12/06/1948
## in Booneville, Mississippi

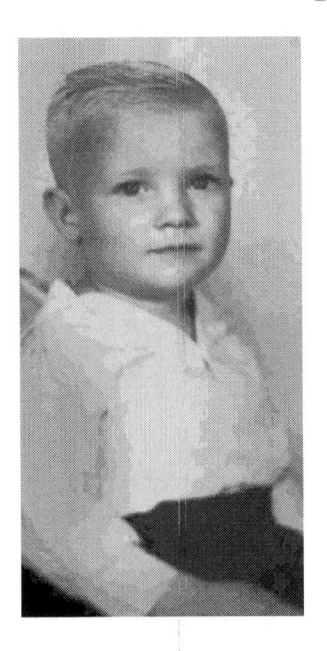

First, a little history about the demographics of my birthplace. As of April 1, 1950, Booneville, Mississippi, located in Prentiss County, had a population of 3,285. Prentiss County had a total population of approximately 7,100. The cross-section of the county's population was 72% white, 21% black, and 7% other, including a small percentage of Native Americans. Prentiss County was named after Sergeant Smith Prentiss.

Sergeant was a first name, not a military rank. Sergeant Prentiss was a Congressman from Natchez, Mississippi. Today, the population of Booneville is approximately 9,300, and Prentiss County's current population is roughly 25,000. The demographic cross-section of the population hasn't significantly changed. Booneville is the county seat of Prentiss County and was named after R.H. Boone, a relative of Daniel Boone.

In the early 1950s, Booneville was a typical, small, rural city. On Saturday afternoons, my grandparents would load us up in the pickup. Avis, my favorite aunt, would sit in the middle of the front seat, and Boyd (my older brother) and I would ride in the truck bed.

PaPa parked near the five & 10 cent store called "the Five and Dime." There were wooden benches located in front of the Five and Dime where the old and young farmers would gather, still in their overalls and Brogans (leather work boots), and discuss everything from the weather, where to get the best moonshine, women, tell jokes and whatever else men tend to talk about.

The men also rolled their own cigarettes from Prince Albert's red tins. They chewed tobacco and dipped snuff. The women would go to the grocery store and the Five and Dime and buy whatever they needed. The key word here is "needed," not "wanted."

They never just bought things we wanted; buying what one wanted was a luxury reserved for those much better off than us. I believe these Saturday afternoon trips to town were a source of entertainment and an opportunity to get off the farm for a few hours.

PaPa would give Boyd and me a quarter each. That was a lot of money for two young boys, such as we were in those days, especially in Mississippi. Boyd and I, without escort, would walk down the street and across the railroad tracks to a small barber shop at the railroad's intersection and a paved street.

The small red and white candy-striped pole out front easily identified this barber shop. The barber knew the two of us, and PaPa had already given him standing orders as to the style of haircut. It wasn't that difficult, expensive, or complicated - we got "buzz" cuts for ten cents each.

Two minutes tops, and we were headed down the street to the local movie theater where for a mere ten cents, we got into a double feature as well as the latest newsreel, and afterward, we still had a nickel for a coke. All soft drinks were referred to as "Coke." You could have a root beer Coke (my favorite) or a Sprite Coke. There was also a chocolate "moo" Coke, etc.

There were no parking meters on the streets at that time in Booneville, and most parking was either parallel or chevron. People only used their vehicle horns to avoid something or someone and never in anger. This was a typical Saturday afternoon for the two of us young boys in Booneville, Mississippi.

My mother once told me a story about the first time her family went to a traveling circus that came to Prentiss County. My mother's younger sister, Juanita (known as "Need"), was very young. When the family walked into the big top tent for the first time, Aunt Need yelled, "My gosh, I didn't know that town had a top on it!" In those days, life in Booneville, Mississippi, was simple and always full of adventure.

One lingering memory from that period of my life: after the haircuts, movies, and a Coke, Boyd and I would go into the Five and Dime to look at all sorts of things that we both knew we could never have. That never stopped us from looking and dreaming.

The most desired material object I ever dreamed of owning was a pocketknife like my grandfather's. While I was inside the store looking and dreaming, PaPa sat outside with the other men whittling on a wood block.

Most of the time, I never knew what, if anything, he was making, and yet he would whittle for hours while talking to the other farmers. I believe that all the men whittled simply to add sawdust to the sidewalk to soak up the tobacco spittle and snuff spit.

He always carried that pocketknife. On a farm, you never knew for what or when you'd need it. Two things he did whittle for Boyd and me were rubber band pistols and slingshot handles…what I wouldn't give to have one of those originals carved by my PaPa.

Years later, my Aunt Avis would give me that knife, and even though I don't carry it everywhere I go, it's one of my most prized possessions and kept in my bookcase along with other things I've collected throughout my life. I'm sure that these little things have absolutely no value to anyone on earth except myself.

# A PARTIAL ALEXANDER FAMILY GENEALOGY

PaPa and MaMa (Read on to learn more about my grandparents).

**Great-Great Grandparents:**

John Robert Alexander: D.O.B. 1829 / D.O.D. 1878
Sarah Elizabeth: D.O.B. 1842 / D.O.D. 1906

**Great-Grandparents:**

Robert Alexander: D.O.B. 1873 / D.O.D. 1911

Mary Rebecca White: D.O.B. 1876 / D.O.D. 1954

(This is the great-grandmother who let me brush her long, black hair.)

**Grandparents:** (My beloved MaMa and PaPa.)

William A. Alexander: D.O.B. 1899 / D.O.D. 1977. Note: His date of birth is approximate. I don't think he or anyone else knew his exact date of birth. He repeatedly told me that he was born in January 1899. His grave marker simply says 1900 – 1977. This was my mother's father, my grandfather, PaPa.

*James Bonapart "Jim" & Eleanor Josephine Belue Goodin Family circa 1907*

James B. "Jim" Goodin

Eleanor Josephine Belue Goodin

John Harvey Goodin appx. 3 yrs old

George Festus Goodin appx 1 yr.

Myrtle appx 5 years old

MaMa's parents. MaMa is on the far right.

Myrtle Goodin: DOB 11/15/1902; DOD 11/29/1971. This was my mother's mother, my grandmother, MaMa.
My older brother Boyd and I lived with these grandparents for most of the first six years of my life. They were always MaMa ("Mam Maw") and PaPa ("Paw Paw") to the two of us.

When Boyd and I lived with them, they lived approximately 4.5 miles south of Booneville, Mississippi, on Osborne Creek Road (a county road). The house was located directly behind or west of the Osborne Creek Baptist Church.

PaPa and MaMa

"Siblings"

Festus Goodin | Myrtle Goodin Alexander | Edna Goodin Wingo | Harvey Goodin

Taken at the home of Elijah & Edna Goodin Wingo
Hatchie Street, Booneville, Mississippi   1964

MaMa's siblings: (L-R) Festus Goodin, Myrtle Goodin Alexander, Edna Goodin Wingo, Harvey Goodin (taken at the home of Elijah and Edna (Goodin) Wingo, 402 Hatchie Street, Booneville, Mississippi, 1964).

LAST WEEKS $200.00 WINNER
MR. W. A. ALEXANDER
ROUTE 2, BOONEVILLE, MISS.

William A. "W.A." Alexander, Jr.
Papa and MaMa's first child and only son.

The following are the children of my PaPa and MaMa (William A. Alexander and Myrtle G. Alexander):

<u>William A. Alexander, Jr.</u>: DOB 1/21/1922; DOD 8/15/1966. (Photo on previous page).

I remember that I was on the football field during practice in Marianna, Arkansas, when someone came to let me know that my Uncle W.A. (pronounced "Dubbie-A") had died from a heart attack while mowing his lawn in Mississippi.

His wife, Virginia, had come out to the shade tree where he was sitting and asked if she could bring him something to drink. She went inside the house to get him a glass of sweet tea (the drink of choice for all Mississippians), and when she came back with the tea, she found him dead.

Uncle W.A. was only 44 years old at his death. He was a successful farmer just outside of Booneville, Mississippi. He was a veteran of WWII.

I was just getting ready to start my senior year of high school, the Class of 1966, at Marianna, Arkansas. An interesting point was that the Marianna High School mascot was the Porcupines. The Junior High School mascot was the Quills. You can't make this stuff up.

<u>Mildred Christine (Alexander) Young, Wells, Yarbrough, and possibly others</u>: DOB 5/30/1924; DOD 9/21/1999.

This was our mother. I said, "possibly others" because I know that she lived with and was the caregiver of an elderly man in Hot Springs, Arkansas, just a few years before her stroke that led to her having to be placed in a nursing home in Hot Springs. I do not recall his name, nor do I know what the relationship was between them.

My mother had several strokes within a few years of her death. The last stroke led to hospitalization in Hot Springs, Arkansas. She spent time in two separate nursing homes in Hot Springs. Eventually, we moved her to a nursing home in Olive Branch, Mississippi, so that she could be close to her sisters living in the area. This was where she lived until she died in 1999.

It does need to be said that she was asked on numerous occasions if she would allow us to have her moved to a facility in Georgia or Washington State, and yet, she adamantly refused. She simply said that she did not like Georgia and that Washington State was simply too far away from her friends and family.

My mother was a VERY strong-willed individual! I may have gotten just a little bit of that from her. I drove to Hot Springs, picked up my mother, and took her to a nursing home in Olive Branch, Mississippi.

That's a 3 1/2 drive and approximately 220 miles. I would not recommend driving an invalid older person under those conditions alone. I'm not sure what I was thinking.

I guess I'm just cheap. I could have and probably should have had her moved by an ambulance. However, I was between wives at the time, and I didn't have much disposable income.

(L-R) Boyd, our Mother, Christine Alexander Young, and me.

May Juanita "Need" (Alexander) Barrett:
DOB 5/30/1927; DOD 10/23/2013.
This was my mother's oldest sister. Most of her life was spent in Booneville, Mississippi, Memphis, Tennessee, and Olive Branch, Mississippi.

Edna Maxine (Alexander) Mink:
DOB 5/20/1931; DOD 11/10/2018.
Jumpertown and Booneville, Mississippi, and Memphis, Tennessee.

Mary Magdalene "Madge" (Alexander) Crabb:
DOB 8/06/1935; DOD 6/14/2003.
Jumpertown and Booneville, Mississippi, Memphis, Tennessee, and Byhalia, Mississippi.

Avis Josephine (Alexander) Hall:
DOB 8/16/1940,
Booneville and Olive Branch, Mississippi.

Avis is, by far, my favorite aunt. She is much more like a big sister than an aunt to me. She has always been my protector, and she gave me hugs when I needed them.
Avis has been exceptionally helpful in capturing a tremendous amount of information for this work that, without her help, I could never have obtained. She deserves an enormous amount of credit for this book. I will love her both on this side, and the other side of eternity.

MaMa and PaPa's children:
Back row: (L) Juanita, (R) Christine/"Chris"
Middle row: (L) Maxine, (R) W. A.
Front row: (L) Avis, (R) Madge.

# A BRIEF YOUNG FAMILY GENEALOGY

John Franklin Young, our grandfather on our father's side.

Our grandparents on our father's side:
<u>John Franklin Young</u>:
DOB 1889; DOD late 1960s.
He was born in Mississippi, and he died in Paden, Mississippi. His life was spent farming.

Emma (Floyd) Young:
DOB 1895; DOD unknown.
She was born in either Oklahoma or Arkansas. The state is on my father's birth certificate, but it's difficult to read. I believe that it was Arkansas. Emma was a homemaker who died in Paden, Mississippi. As of this date, I've done very little concerning an ancestry search on the Young side of the family. However, a few years back, my wife gave me a DNA kit.

I sent it off, and according to it, I had almost no Native American DNA I mention this only because my grandmother Young told me that her mother was half Native American. That would have been an easy claim to accept if you had seen my grandmother. The truth is that I really don't know. The entire thing leaves me questioning the validity of DNA tests delivered via the US mail. Hopefully, through further discovery and research, we'll learn more about this side of the family

These are the children of my Young grandparents. (Note that these may not be in the order of birth).

Hynton Carliss Young:
DOB 5/16/1926; DOD 5/09/1989.
This is our father. Dad's birth certificate spells his first name "Hinton," while his death certificate says "Hynton." Dad was born in Paden, Mississippi, and died in Augusta, Georgia.

Faye (Young) Mann
Jewel (Young) Mann
Maxine (Young) South
Luther Young
Lester Young
Clayton Young
Eva (Young) Bryant
Tressie (Young) Painter

<u>Willodean "Dean" (Young) Abler</u>
<u>Coolidge Young</u>

As of the publication of this book, I have no information on the birth and death dates of children #s 2-11. There are cemetery research sites all over the internet. We could track them down if it is essential to know. I intend to follow up on these dates, and I may have these shown twice under different names.

My father's wives (of which I am aware):

Mildred "Christine" (Alexander) Young, Wells, and Yarbrough: (my mother). DOB 5/30/1924 in Booneville, Mississippi, DOD 9/19/1999 in Olive Branch, Mississippi.

Agnes" Mae (Swims) Wilson, Young: (my stepmother) DOB 12/20/1921 in Amagon, Arkansas, DOD 10/08/2002 in Augusta, Georgia.

My siblings:

Boyd Hynton Young: DOB 11/17/1947 in Booneville, Mississippi; DOD: 8/19/2004 in Seattle, Washington.

Debra (Deb) Guinn (Wells) Lambert, Sais: DOB 5/12/1955 in Memphis, Tennessee, currently living in Belen, New Mexico.

Jorden (Jay) Conrad Wells, III: DOB 9/24/1961, in Memphis, Tennessee, currently living in Belen, New Mexico.

Billie Steve Wilson: DOB 8/06/1946 in Balch, Arkansas, DOD 03/19/2024, in Meridian, Idaho. This is my stepbrother. He is the son of my stepmother, Agnes Young. I do consider him my brother, even though we have no blood connection.

Billie Steve and I never spent much time together. However, we have had some memorable times.

<u>Sharon Ann (Wilson) Langston</u>: DOB 2/21/1944, in Newport, Arkansas, currently living in Augusta, Georgia.

    Sharon's husband is Melvin "Mel" Ray Langston, born March 10, 1943, in Newark, Arkansas. Sharon is the daughter of my stepmother, Agnes Young. We have no blood connection, and yet, Sharon has been a true sister to me since about the time I entered the Marine Corps.

    The defining moment of our lifelong relationship began, at least for me, when I returned from Vietnam. I pulled up in front of my dad and stepmom's house in Harlem, Georgia (just outside of Augusta), and Sharon came running out of the house crying and basically jumped into my arms. She cried and held on for what seemed like forever. She just kept saying, "Boyce, I've prayed and prayed and prayed that you'd come home safely." She is and will always be my sister.

My wives:
Diane Medders Young Davis: DOB 12/26/1951 in Savannah, Georgia. She and I married on 12/07/1973 and divorced in early 1980.

Deborah (Debby) Louise Williams Young Jones: DOB 11/30/1960 in Hardeeville, South Carolina. She and I were married on 4/18/1980 and divorced in August 1992.

Eva Dianne Hogan Herrington Young: DOB 11/26/1950 in Savannah, Georgia. She and I married on 12/05/1998.

There's a pattern shaping up here: Diane, Debby, and Dianne. I appear to have this thing with women whose names begin with a "D."

My children:
Christopher Mark (Smith) Young:
DOB 1/18/1972, in Savannah, Georgia.
Chris is the son of my first wife, Diane Medders.
I adopted Chris in 1974. I have no information on his father. Chris' mother and father were never married. The only information I have on Chris' birth father is that he was from Savannah, Georgia.

Kimberly Joanna Young Patterson: DOB 6/03/1975, in Savannah, Georgia, currently living in Brunswick, Georgia.
Kimberly is married to Kevin Patterson.
Kimberly's mother is Diane Medders. Kimberly has three children, Katelyn (Patterson) Allen, Keaton

Patterson, and Kyle Patterson, and one granddaughter, Bonnie Allen, born to Katelyn and her husband Grant on 2/15/2022 (my first great-granddaughter).

Kimberly has been and continues to be my stronghold and my strongest supporter during thick and thin since June 3, 1975. She's not perfect, yet I'm not sure I would have survived without her support. She has been a source of spiritual strength and encouragement to me all her life.

One of my most beloved memories of Kimberly was on the day that I left her mom. I had loaded everything I owned into the cab of my 1976 Toyota truck shown in the photo on following page. I was sitting in the truck crying. Kimberly came to the truck dressed in tiny orange shorts and a yellow halter top and kissed me.

She placed her hands on her hips, looked up at me, and said, "Don't cry, Daddy; everything will be alright." This was before Bob Marley's famous song. This was in early 1980, and Kimberly wasn't yet five years old. She comes across as a softy, yet I know she has the heart of a mother lion. She has, indeed, been a true gift from God to me.

I recall when Dennis Hutton (one of the sons of Mr. Joseph Hutton, one of the founders of Thomas & Hutton Engineering Co.) and I were working in McRae, Georgia, performing a twenty-four-hour continuous flow test on the wastewater system for the city of McRae. The test began at midnight, Sun., June 1, 1975, and continued through midnight, Monday, June 2, 1975.

You can only imagine how dirty and sweaty Dennis and I were after climbing in and out of one-hundred-year- old manholes to get a flow reading every hour on the hour for twenty-four continuous hours.

When we finished the testing, we drove back to the office in Savannah. When I walked in the door at Thomas & Hutton Engineering Company's office on Bay Street, one of the receptionists asked me if I was aware that my wife (first wife) was in the hospital delivering our baby.

Obviously, I was not; this was many years before the mobile phone I sped home, took a quick shower, and got to the hospital with only minutes to spare before Kimberly Joanna Young was born. She was my first child, a little girl, and I was in love with her from the first moment I saw her. I've been told that her middle name (Joanna) means "A Gift from God." Nothing could be more accurate.

Kimberly was born in the old Telfair Hospital in Savannah, Georgia. This was basically a birthing hospital where things were done the old-fashioned way. Fathers weren't allowed in the delivery room during the birth, and they were not allowed to touch the newborn baby for three days.

My first look at Kimberly was through a glass wall. Someone had to point out which baby was mine. I am sure that I had tears of gratitude in my eyes as I looked at her. Many years later, I held a six-year-old Kimberly looking through a similar nursery window at her new baby brother, Boyce Leslie Young, Jr.

Boyce L. Young, Jr.: DOB 4/24/1981, in Savannah, Georgia, currently living in Thunderbolt, Georgia. Boyce is married to Anna (Moody) Young. Boyce's mother is Deborah (Debby) Louise Williams (my second wife). Boyce, Jr., and Anna have two children, Cameron Rader Young, and Boyce "Bo" Leslie Young, III.

Boyce, Jr. was a surprise; his mother and I had not intended to have children until we were married for a few years. Boyce, Jr. was born on the twenty-fourth of April, one year and six days after his mom and I were married......SURPRISE!

Boyce's mom had intended to have her baby naturally. We went to all the classes, practiced everything at home and classes held at the hospital, and had the process down to a fine art. Unlike when Kimberly was born, I was not only allowed in the delivery room, but I was also an active participant. Things had really changed in six short years. Boyce Jr. was born at the Candler/Telfair Hospital on DeRenne Avenue, Savannah, Georgia.

When we arrived at the hospital in an old pick-up truck, just as we entered the parking lot, Boyce's mother's water broke. I thought, "Damn, there went my truck seat!" I dropped her off at the emergency room entrance and parked the truck (with its freshly wet seat). I got inside just in time to be rushed into labor and delivery.

Once I got into labor and delivery, this entire process took much longer than I thought it would, but finally, Boyce, Jr. entered this world. I was standing beside the delivery bed holding Boyce's mom's hand, and as soon as Boyce, Jr. appeared, the doctor handed him to me and instructed me to keep his face as close as I could to my own.

I did so and looked deeply into his eyes for a long time. At this time, Boyce's umbilical cord was still attached to his mom. It still gives me great pleasure to know that the first family member Boyce, Jr. saw "on this side" was me.

The doctor cut the umbilical cord while I was holding him. This was an unimaginable pleasure. I highly recommend this to anyone who has not experienced it. I could easily author a book about any of my children, but I won't. I will say that Boyce, Jr. took his approach to life as he played basketball and football. If there was no blood, "How the Hell could it have been called a foul?"

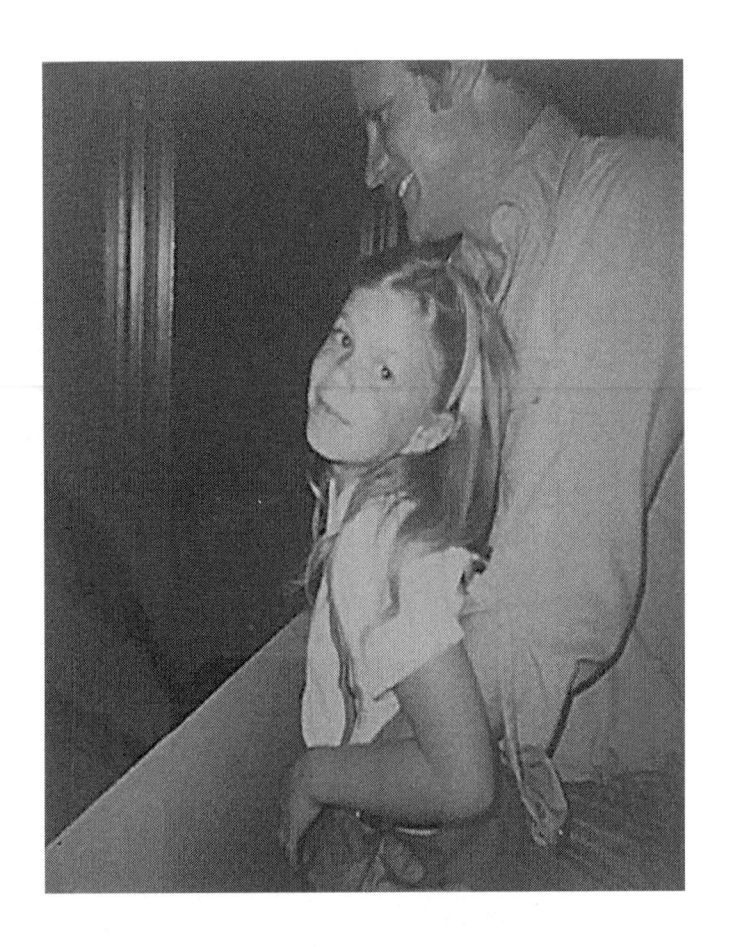

Me holding Kimberly as we look at the newly born Boyce L. Young, Jr. through the hospital's nursery window.

(L) Boyce L. Young holding Byron C. Young,

(R) Boyd H. Young with Boyce L. Young, Jr. in Seattle, WA, 1986.

(L-R) Boyce L. Young, Jr., Boyce L. Young, Sr., and Anna (Moody) Young, December 31, 2019.

<u>Byron Carliss Young</u>: DOB 4/19/1985 in Savannah, Georgia.

Byron is married to Carrie (Poss) Young. Byron's mother is Deborah (Debby) Louise Williams. Byron and Carrie have three daughters, Emily, Ellis, and Mae, and a son, Hyton Webb Young, born December 31, 2022.

Truth be told, Hyton may have been a last-minute tax deduction for Byron and Carrie. The two of them are obviously very brave young parents. Byron and his family currently live in Toccoa, GA.

Byron is unique among my children; he was the only one who was planned. His mom and I wanted him to be our last and wanted him to be born on our wedding anniversary.

Our fifth anniversary was April 18, 1985; Byron was born on April 19, 1985. Someone obviously screwed up…it had to be his mom. That's my story, and I'm sticking to it!

During Byron's birth, I was also in the labor and delivery room as an active participant. When Byron was born, the doctor handed me this tiny boy with his umbilical cord still attached. Once again, my instructions were clear: hold your son close to your face, and once his face is washed off, the first thing that he would see was his daddy's face. The only thing different with Byron was that the doctor also gave me a pair of surgical scissors and instructed me as to where to cut the umbilical cord.

I was expecting the cord to be somewhat flexible, and tender---it wasn't. It felt more like a water hose and took a little more effort to cut it than I was expecting. Cutting the umbilical cord gave me a sensation I'd never felt before or since. It was a once-in-a-lifetime experience that I'll never forget.

It was like I was saying, "Son, you are no longer dependent upon your mother for life. Dad is now here to help raise and nurture you." This was, most certainly, a Divine experience. And yet, it was also a realization of a tremendous lifelong responsibility.

I genuinely believe that this is the point where God said to me, "Pass what you've learned on to your children." I have strived to do that to the best of my ability. Byron was just as athletic as Boyce, Jr., just not quite as savage.

Byron could have received an athletic scholarship from several colleges, and yet, he only wanted to go to the University of Georgia (UGA). He graduated from UGA in 2009. He and Boyce are both still very active in athletics and especially golf.

Byron C. Young's Club Championship Marker, Curahee Country Club, Toccoa, GA.

Boyce L. Young holding Byron C. Young, Boyce L. Young Jr., in front.

<u>Alison Renee' (Herrington) Hand</u>: DOB 10/04/1974 in Savannah, Georgia, currently living in Yakima, Washington.

Alison is my stepdaughter, the daughter of Dianne (my third wife) and David Herrington. Alison is married to Park Hand. Alison is a Registered Nurse and spent fifteen years as a flight nurse on a medical helicopter. She and I agreed early in my marriage to her mother that we didn't like the concept of "stepdaughter." So, we settled on the titles of "Para-daughter" and "Para-dad."

Alison's father passed away at age 29. He had diabetes and succumbed to that condition. Alison was only five and a half at the time. The first time I met Alison was when her dad passed. Her mother worked at Thomas & Hutton Engineering Co. when our office was located on Factors Walk near Bay Street in downtown Savannah.

Alison would come in after school or dance class and spend time with her mom until she got off work. At a very young age, Alison was very independent and
just a little bit sassy. I was still married to my first wife, Diane Medders, at the time. After her mom and I were married, I began to refer to Diane and Dianne as "Di one" and "Di two," and, of course, there was a Debby thrown in the middle.

Many years and two ex-wives later, when Alison's mom and I started dating, Alison disapproved. By this time, Alison was a grown woman and did not want to share her mom with anyone. Over time, she and I grew close, and all those old feelings went out the window. Most of the time, to avoid confusion, I'll simply introduce Alison as my daughter.

By now, you can see that I have had a propensity to be married more than just once. Honestly, I believe that was due to my early philosophy of "three dates, and you're out" that you will read about later. Most likely, it's simply because I never learned how to develop, nurture, and strengthen relationships. I accept full responsibility for that.

Alison on duty as a Registered Flight Nurse.

Alison in Melissa Cottle Semken's (first cousin) wedding.

# 1948 – 1949
## Booneville, Mississippi

I was born in Booneville, Mississippi at the community clinic, on Monday, December 6, 1948. According to my mother, I weighed in at 3 lbs. and ten ounces. Of course, I have no memory of this time of my life, and yet, my Grandfather Alexander (PaPa) was the one who gave me the nickname "Pee-Wee." According to my PaPa, when he looked at me for the first time as a newborn, he shook his head and said, "Pee-Wee, you'll never make it in this big world."

He told me later that he never expected me to survive. I suppose I've always been a little hardheaded and was determine to prove him and others wrong. I hated this nickname from as far back as I can remember. I tried to discourage family members from calling me by that nickname, and for the most part, I was somewhat successful.

On a recent trip (November 2021) to visit relatives in Mississippi, my first cousin, Jerry Barrett, referred to me by that nickname. I think I may have hurt his feelings when I ignored his greeting to me because he was using that nickname. If so, I hope that he will forgive me. Jerry has always been one of my favorite male cousins, and I've always deeply respected him.

In their defense, that nickname is all they had ever known me by during our younger years, and we've not spent a great amount of time together since my going into the Marine Corps at age nineteen in 1968. Also, it's worth mentioning that Jerry's sister, Oretta (Rita), was my first serious crush. I was very young, and I'm sure that she never knew I had a crush on her...I thought she was "drop-dead gorgeous." That's Mississippi for "Damn, she was beautiful!" Rita passed away a few years ago.

At family reunions and other family gatherings, my kinfolks persisted in calling me "Pee-Wee." One by one, I offended them all by insisting that they should call me "Boyce" and only "Boyce." From time to time, I guess I must still remind them.

It is strange, and yet, as I get older, that nickname doesn't offend me as much as it did in the past. I still would prefer not to be known as Pee-Wee but being called that doesn't hurt as much as it once did. I have to say this, being called "Pee-Wee" by my PaPa and MaMa was perfectly okay. It was only after I began school and was criticized by other kids that I began hating the nickname.

Thanks, PaPa. I know that you meant no harm, and I still love you more than life. Oh, and by the way, I also miss you. I'm looking forward, with great anticipation, to seeing you and spending a lot of time with you on the other side. That nickname most likely taught me how to fight and stand up for myself. Let's call it "PaPa's Life Survival Lesson 101."

# 1949 – 1950
## Houston, Texas

Obviously, I have no memory of this time in my life. So, I'll have to rely on my memory of what my mother and grandmother told me in later years. Apparently, my mother and father moved to the Houston, Texas area when I was just a baby, and my older brother, Boyd, was a toddler. I have no earthly idea why they chose to move to Texas or what, if any, connection they had in that part of the country.

Regardless of the reasons they moved, things certainly didn't work out the way they had planned. Shortly after the move, my mother, brother, and I boarded a train from Houston to Memphis and then a Greyhound bus from Memphis to Booneville, Mississippi. Our parents divorced. My mother moved to Memphis to find some sort of employment. I'm uncertain of what kind of job my mother found there. I can only assume that it was as a waitress. The only occupations I was aware of my mother practicing were waitressing and housekeeping.

Boyd and I were left with my mother's parents in Booneville. I'm not sure what my father was doing during this time. I know that he eventually re-enlisted in the U.S. Army. I don't ever remember seeing him again until I was twelve years old. I know that my father had been in the Army during World War II and had spent time in Germany.

Dad spent a total of twenty-eight years in the Army, with a total of six years in Germany, six years in Korea, and three one- year tours of duty in Vietnam. Dad's first tour of duty in Vietnam was at the same base as my brother Boyd. His second tour was during the same year that I was in Vietnam, and we were based only about 120 miles apart.

His third and last tour of duty in Vietnam was in 1972 or 1973. He did this tour of duty "in country" (Vietnam) by himself. Whether or not his military service was the reason we moved from Mississippi to Texas, I will never know. However, when my mother was in the later stage of her pregnancy with me, our house in Paden, Mississippi, burned to the ground.

My parents may have simply decided to start fresh elsewhere. I've always had a birthmark around my navel that looks very similar to flames. My mother was convinced that it was the result of the house fire. I've never been that superstitious. I think it was simply a sloppy removal of the umbilical cord, which left a scar.

# 1949-1956
## Booneville, Mississippi
## (1955-1956-first grade)

I do not recall when Boyd and I first arrived at our grandparents' home in Booneville, Mississippi, and yet, some of my most treasured memories of growing up were while we were living with my MaMa and PaPa Alexander.

Those memories only grew as we spent the summers with them for most of our early years. My mothers' parents were sharecroppers in the very rural areas near Booneville, Jumpertown (Jumpertown was named after the Jumper family), Corinth, Iuka, and Sleek Creek Hollow, Mississippi. You can't make these names up; they are real towns and communities in northeast Mississippi. That's my story, and I'm sticking to it!

For the most part, we lived about five miles south of Booneville, Mississippi, on a county road named Osborne Creek Road.

For the benefit of those who don't know what a sharecropper is: it is simply someone who works the land of a wealthy landowner. Usually, the wealthy landowner provided a house, barn, garden spot, and possibly some pasture space for the sharecropper to raise most of his own food.

The sharecropper farms the landowner's land. Seed, fertilizer, farm equipment, etc., are provided by the landowner. The sharecropper only gets a small portion of the profit from the crop. This was an extremely hard life, and it was almost impossible to get out of the rut once one was in it.

With that said, it's the only life that my grandparents ever knew. For PaPa, with only a third-grade education, there was little else available for him to do to make a living in rural Mississippi.

Of course, at the young age that Boyd and I came to live with our grandparents, we never knew that we were poor. All we really knew was that there were unlimited places to play in the woods, in the fields, ride the livestock, swim in the creek or the pond, etc.

This was a young boy's dream come true. That includes when we worked in the fields. We were expected to do so, even at a very early age. We weeded the field rows using a hoe, chopped, and picked cotton the old-fashioned way, by hand, and dragged a cotton sack behind us.

My Aunt Avis would throw a handful of cotton in my sack from time to time. Even at that very young age, my grandfather had a certain weight that he expected Boyd and me to achieve during a day of picking.

We would drag our sacks to the back of the wagon where my grandfather would record in a field notebook the totals for each picker. When we got to the gin with the cotton, he would check his total with the gin keeper's scales. The two would almost certainly match. These are very sweet memories, especially my Aunt Avis helping me meet my expected quota.

The only time that I can ever remember my grandfather giving me a whipping (known as a "whooping" in Mississippi) was when he gave Boyd and me each a nickel. One of our jobs was to ride on top of the cotton in the trailer on the way to the gin to keep as much cotton as possible from blowing out. It was a blast for two young boys to ride way up high, looking down on cars and trucks passing us on the highway.

We thought we were in the "big time." These days, my grandfather would probably be put in jail for endangering the lives of young children. Somehow, I lost my nickel while riding to the gin.

Normally, this wouldn't have been a problem, except the gin removed the cotton from the trailer using a huge vacuum. The cotton was sucked out of the trailer after the entire thing was weighed, and then it was sent through fancy deseeding devices. Well, the nickel (which, obviously, wasn't nickel at all) created a spark in the machinery, and this caused a fire. Fortunately, the fire was very small and was extinguished quickly, and yet, my PaPa was not a happy camper.

He and the gin keeper quickly determined the cause of the fire and asked Boyd and me for our nickels. Boyd produced his first and I searched my pockets to no avail. PaPa produced the dented nickel and I think I may have wet my pants.

It's a good thing that the cotton had been removed from the wagon or it would have gotten very wet. PaPa took me behind the gin and proceeded to blister my backside with a switch because his overalls didn't have a belt. I don't know which one of us cried the most... him or me.

In hindsight, his entire year's work could have quickly gone up in smoke, not to mention the cost of the damage to the cotton gin. I think that he realized that I did not lose my nickel intentionally. After all, a nickel was a fortune to me then, yet his first reaction was anger. I think, indirectly, that he taught me a very important life lesson: I've always tended to have a bad temper. However, it takes a lot to get me to that breaking point.

A cotton gin similar to the one I inadvertently tried to burn down with my lost nickel.

# PICKING BLACKBERRIES AND EATING MAMA'S TEA CAKES

I remember that PaPa and MaMa had a blackberry patch in the pasture directly behind the house. I was very young and very small; after all, I was "Pee-Wee," and MaMa would place me in a #3 galvanized metal wash tub and place the tub and me as far as she could reach into the patch.

I was lightweight enough that I wouldn't sink very deeply into the briars. I would pick as far as I could reach, and then she would move the tub and me, and we'd keep that up until we had the patch picked clean. My grandmother was a short and round woman. When she moved me, she would get tickled and laugh from her head to her toes.

I don't know exactly how old I was, and yet, I couldn't have been more than 2-3 years old at the time, and how much could a "Pee-Wee" weigh?

The memories of blackberry picking with MaMa have always very sweet. I don't think I feared the briars. However, the possibility of snakes scared the bejesus out of me.

My grandmother was an awesome cook, as most women of her time were. She used to fix "tea cakes," a thin cookie. I do not know, to this day, exactly what was in those cookies. However, I can tell you, for sure, that the ingredients included pure vanilla extract, butter, eggs, buttermilk, and pure cane sugar. If you Google (this is a term used in the 2000's for searching the Internet) "Old-Fashioned Southern Tea Cakes," you will find many recipes.

MaMa's tea cake recipe originated due to the time and place in which they lived. They made "do" with the ingredients they had. As www.lanascooking.com website states, "There's nothing at all fancy in this recipe…they simply used what they had on hand. Very smart and frugal folks!"

When MaMa was mixing those delicious tea cakes, Boyd and I would sit around the kitchen table with drool falling off our lips, just waiting, in anticipation of licking the wooden spoon that she used to mix the cookie dough.

Yes, the dough was raw. It was an unbelievable treat for two young country boys. By the way, we licked the same spoon, and I don't think either of us ever got sick, nor was our growth stunted. Pee-Wee now weighs around 225 pounds and is six' 2" tall. Boyd was a much larger man than me.

Keep in mind that almost everything we ate came from the farm. Boyd and I both churned butter in a #4 butter churn like the one pictured on the next page. Note: our home-churned butter was white in color…not the yellow of today's butter.

Southern Tea Cakes

A galvanized metal washtub similar to my transportation down the blackberry patch with MaMa.

48

# KITTY SICKLES AND SWITCHES

During one of my mother's visits to see Boyd and me, I remember the weather being very cold---below freezing. We always had farm cats around the house and barn; these cats had a purpose: they managed the mice and rat population. One day, one of these cats had six kittens. Boyd and I got to the kittens shortly after they were born. You must understand these kittens were very dirty.

Boyd and I had watched my grandmother wash clothes using a traditional scrub board in that #3 washtub. So, in our infinite wisdom, we filled the wash tub with water and soap and gave those kittens a proper bath. Then we hung them on the barbed wire fence (using clothes pins, of course) as neither of us could reach the clothesline.

As boys will do, we got distracted and went off exploring other parts of the farm. Sometime later, we heard our mother screaming our names. We ran to the house only to find her standing by six "kitty-sickles." She ordered us to each go cut a switch. Her exact instructions were: "If it is not big enough, you do not want me to get one." Boyd apparently found one that met Mom's specifications; I obviously didn't.

While Boyd was getting his tail torn up, I proceeded to climb the tallest tree that I could find. It was my plan never to come down, or at least not until my mom had gone back to Memphis.

Well, she sat down on the ground and leaned against the tree that I had climbed, and it turned out that she could wait a lot longer than I could cling to that tree.

A traditional galvanized wash bucket in which we washed the dirty kittens.

Finally, I crept down, and she had, indeed, found a switch that met her approval. I don't remember her crying, and yet, I'm not sure that I stopped until she was back in Memphis.

MaMa, PaPa, Avis, Boyd, and I lived in a three room (including the kitchen) house built of unpainted plank siding with unfinished plank floors and a tin roof. This house was located directly behind a brick church, the Osborne Creek Baptist Church.

The parking lot for this church was packed with red clay. This clay was as hard as concrete when it was dry and yet, when wet, it was as slick as an ice-skating rink. Boyd and I played on that clay parking lot regularly.

Our clothes were never clean again. We learned to ride a neighbor's bike on that clay parking lot. We tried to ride a pogo stick on it…that didn't work out so well.

This po-go stick belonged to a girl who lived a short distance away down the paved Osborne Creek Road that ran in front of the church. I think her name was Joann Richardson. We thought these people were super rich. After all, they lived in a brick house with finished hardwood floors, and it was probably at least 1,000 square feet of living space.

Are you beginning to get the picture now? Yes, Boyd and I decided that the hardwood floors would work much better for the pogo stick than the clay parking lot. It worked very well; however, the rubber tip on the bottom of the pogo stick had long since worn off, and the hardwood floors did not survive.

Once again, I got my backside blistered. It was worse this time because I had to wait a couple of weeks for my mother to come visit from Memphis. I grew to hate it when my mother would come to visit. I think my grandfather refused to spank me on her behalf after the cotton gin issue.

Osborne Creek Baptist Church, present day.

On another occasion, one of our hens had just hatched a few new little yellow chicks. Boyd and I played with the little chicks most of one day, and when it became to go in and get ready for supper and bed, Boyd and I came up with a brilliant idea.

To this day, I believe that it was Boyd's idea, and I am certain that I tried to talk him out of it. Should you choose to believe that I have some Alpine property located in Miami that I'd love to let you have at a great price. At least, "That's my story, and I'm sticking to it." (Boyd, please forgive me in the unlikely event that I'm mistaken.)

Our brilliant idea was to put the chicks under a shoe box and place the box outside our bedroom window. We theorized that this would save time the next day. After all, it took considerable effort to catch those newborn chicks, especially with their momma trying her best to eat us alive to protect them. Early the next morning, our MaMa found the shoebox and the dead chicks (apparently, they needed oxygen to survive).

MaMa cut a switch (much smaller than the one PaPa found at the cotton gin), then she brought us both outside to see the chicks and asked us, "Which one of you boys did this?" She said that if the guilty one didn't own up to it, she was going to whoop us both.

I was obviously just a little bit slow in the head and I quickly raised my hand and confessed to the crime to save one of us from that dreaded switch.

I never gave a thought to the fact that I was the one that would be getting the whooping. By this time, Boyd was walking off into the sunset, once again. I got my whooping.

An interesting, random memory: Growing up in rural Mississippi at this time, whenever one child in the family had the mumps, measles, chicken pox, etc., the other children were made to sleep in the same bed with the sick one. This would ensure that the other children would catch the same virus and the entire ordeal would soon be over. I'm not sure why I made a big deal of that memory...Boyd and I slept in the same bed anyway until I was fourteen.

The Osborne Creek Road was paved and ran north and south to the east of the Osborne Creek Baptist Church. Just south of the church was a dirt (red clay) road that ran west. Our house was on the north side of the dirt road directly behind the church, maybe a hundred yards or so away.

Located in the southwest corner of this intersection was a very old two-room schoolhouse. One room in this schoolhouse was for grades 1-6, and the other room was for grades 7-12. Located directly behind and to the west of the schoolhouse were two outhouses or "privies"). One was marked "boys" and the other "girls," after all, we were "civilized." The schoolhouse didn't have indoor plumbing or running water.

There was a hand-pump where the students filled metal buckets and took them into the schoolhouse. Everyone used the same tin dipper to drink from the buckets. I don't know how we could have possibly survived such conditions... (That's a joke.)

The summer before I was to start the 1st grade, this school was closed. I really wanted to start school here and that was one of my very first huge disappointments. I really liked the idea of going to school directly across the dirt road from my MaMa. That's another story.

There was an old lady (of course, she may have been 30 years old) who always wore very old and ragged clothes. She carried a walking stick and a bag; I think the bag was an old pillowcase. We didn't know her, and yet, Boyd and I seriously thought that she was a witch. One day, Boyd and I were playing around the old, now closed, schoolhouse.

We had climbed up on top of the two outhouses. How we got up there, I will never know. Suddenly, Boyd yelled, "Here comes the witch!" I looked up in fear. Reflecting on her movement as an adult, she was probably coming towards us to attempt to prevent us from killing ourselves.

However, when I heard the words, "Here comes the witch," I jumped off the outhouse and landed on a two-by-four with a rusty nail pointing straight up. The nail went as far into my foot as it could go.

I felt no pain. I was scared. Again, I most likely wet my pants. I ran all the way home with that two-by- four stuck to my foot. Boyd reached the house before me, only because he wasn't limping along with a two- by-four attached to his foot. He and MaMa came running to meet me. MaMa was screaming, and yet, she never slowed down.

She placed her feet on the board and pulled my foot free. She took me inside, washed my foot, and put either mercurochrome or Merthiolate (the popular first aid antiseptics at the time, probably both containing pure mercury) in the hole.

I never went to the doctor, never got a tetanus shot, and, as far as I know, I never developed any sort of infection. I suppose that God looks out for "Dumb Ass Country Boys from Mississippi" (DACBFM).

Once the old two-room schoolhouse closed, it was obvious that I would have to go elsewhere for my first year of school. My favorite aunt, even to this day, was Avis. Avis was eight years older than me, and she was my protector. She was and still is my favorite aunt because of the six years that we lived together; we are more like siblings than nephew and aunt.

On my first day of school, that BIG yellow bus pulled up on that red clay parking lot in front of our house and that was a very long walk for a young boy who really didn't want to go anywhere other than the large white two-room schoolhouse across the road from our house.

In my mind, I simply could not understand why the Mississippi Board of Education couldn't reopen that simple schoolhouse, especially for Pee-Wee.

That did not happen. With my grandmother pushing me, ignoring my cries of headache, fever, stomachache, and possibly an infection from that nail,

I boarded the bus while crying my eyes out. The other kids had absolutely no mercy for me. They were making fun of the "cry baby."

My aunt Avis, who was already on the bus, stood up, and I'm not sure exactly what she said, and yet, it worked, you could hear a pin drop, and none of the kids ever bothered me again. I doubt that Aunt Avis remembers what she said. However, I'm reasonably sure that she would not have wanted MaMa or PaPa to have heard it. It may have scared me enough to stop my crying.

The new school that the Mississippi State Board of Education decided that I should attend was in the small community of Wheeler, Mississippi. Wheeler was maybe five miles from where we lived. And yet, for Pee-Wee, riding on that big yellow school bus, it seemed like a hundred miles away.

To make matters worse, after we got to the new school, and I had no more tears to shed, we had this thing called "recess." Now, with this thing called "recess," I was beginning to enjoy school a bit more until I walked under a swing set, got knocked in the head and was laid out, unconscious. That incident is a pretty good metaphor for my school career for the next twelve years.

The school in Wheeler, Mississippi, was the first of twenty-two different schools located in thirteen states that I would attend before joining the Marine Corps. There were eight different high schools and fourteen different elementary and middle schools.

Sometime during these early school days (I'm not sure if it was before or after starting school), Boyd and I snuck through the woods behind our house to a cemetery located a few hundred yards north of the church.

Of course, we had been told by MaMa and PaPa to never go to the cemetery (which was located just north of the church.) We were also required to be home before dark.

It was not dark when we started toward the cemetery, and I'm reasonably sure we didn't intend to enter it. However, it was very dark when we reached the fence around the cemetery. We saw a lamp somewhere in the cemetery, and, as boys will do, we had to huddle down and see if we could tell what was happening.

I don't think Boyd and I were ever able to determine why a light was shining in the cemetery. However, a few days later, we overheard MaMa and PaPa talking about how some grave robbers were caught red-handed. Boyd and I never went back.

Of course, in our simple little minds, we thought the robbers were stealing bodies---only heaven knew for what purpose. We never gave a thought to the robbers simply wanting whatever valuables might have been buried with the bodies, such as wedding rings, watches, etc.

During this period of my life, there were very large, ugly turtles in this area of Mississippi. The locals called them "loggerheads." I later learned that they were "alligator snapping turtles." These turtles were extremely aggressive and could inflict serious injury on anyone, so Boyd and I gave them a lot of respect.

The fear was most likely exaggerated in our minds from the stories that our grandfather told us about these turtles dragging young boys off into the woods and never being heard from again.

If you're poor and live in rural Mississippi, you can learn to eat about anything that walks, crawls, flies, swims, etc. I assume that's true no matter where you live and are poor.

My grandmother could make stew from almost anything, and alligator snapping turtles were no exception. Unless you've tried it, don't knock it. She taught Boyd and me to find a long, strong stick should we encounter one of these critters while we were exploring.

The longer the stick, the better. She taught us to poke the stick in front of the turtle and, most of the time, if not every time, the turtle would reach to bite down on the stick. Once the turtle had bitten down on the stick, they simply would not let go. Boyd and I did this on several occasions.

When MaMa saw us dragging a turtle down the old dirt road, she would start smiling and run to get the axe. We would simply drag the turtle to an old wood chopping block and pull its head over it. MaMa took care of the rest.

She cleaned the turtle, added it and every vegetable known to man into a large pot. After it had cooked for several hours, she would "fix" (that's Southern for "cook" or "prepare") a well-seasoned cast iron skillet full of cornbread, and we had a feast! I'm sure she used a lot of home-grown seasonings. I wasn't privileged to know those details.

She also made a delicious catfish head stew. The same process as described above was used only using the discarded heads of catfish. Of course, the catfish bodies would have been fried for a different meal. In rural Mississippi, no part of any animal was wasted. When we slaughtered pigs, my PaPa used to say, "The only part of the pig that we don't eat is the squeal."

One other Mississippi delicacy was chitlins. Chitlins may be better described as "Shitlins." Chitlins are the large intestines of a pig. I guess, technically, it could be the large intestine of any animal. All we ever used was the gut of a slaughtered pig.

The process of making chitlins was simple. You simply removed the pig's intestines (I'm assuming you know that the pig was dead at this point), turned them inside out, washed them thoroughly, cut them into the desired length (about 1-inch max), and you had chitlins.

Most of the time, we had them fried (frying is, after all, the "Southern way"). I've known people to boil them with other ingredients to make a chitlin stew. My grandmother would make cornbread and include fried chitlins...yum, yum! They were not bad eaten like you would eat fried pork skins today.

"Cracklins" were very similar to chitlins, except they were made using the pig's skin. It was also common to eat cracklins by themselves, fried, of course, or to be cooked in cornbread. The fried pork skins that you buy in the store today are basically cracklins.

We also ate the ears, nose, jaws, tail (the curly thing), and feet. The feet were pickled just like cucumbers.

# SNUFF & STUFF

MaMa and PaPa were products of their place and time. Most country people in Mississippi during the time my grandparents lived had bad habits much the same as we do today. My MaMa and PaPa were no different. Both of them dipped snuff.

In the possibility that the reader doesn't know what snuff is: it's simply a finely pulverized tobacco that can be drawn up into the nostrils by inhaling or simply be placed under the tongue to allow it to be slowly absorbed into the bloodstream. I'm assuming that this gives one a high, sort of like smoking tobacco. I personally have never tried using the real thing.

In those days, you could (and maybe still can today) buy snuff in small metal cans that contained maybe a quarter of a cup, or you could buy it in very large containers. The small containers were easy to carry on one's person, and the amount contained therein was apparently a day's worth of snuff.

They would use the old tin containers repeatedly until they wore them out, filling them from the large container each morning.

During Boyd and my summer visits to our grandparents, my grandmother would give each of us one of these small, worn-out snuff cans. We would proceed to fill the cans with a mixture of powdered cocoa and sugar.

We would pretend it was snuff, carry it in the back pocket of our worn-out three-time hand-me- down blue jeans, and walk around spitting with the best of them. Once again, we thought we were "big time."

Boyd and I were also notorious for raiding our neighbor's watermelon and cantaloupe patches. We always carried a saltshaker (also made from an old snuff can) in the other back pocket.

We would clandestinely sneak into the watermelon/cantaloupe patch, grab a couple, and run into the nearby woods. We would bust the melons open on a log or anything sharp that we could find, eat the melon with our bare hands, using a generous portion of salt, and making sure to not confuse the "snuff" for the salt.

After we had gorged ourselves, we'd go to the nearest creek or pond and swim with our clothes on. We had to wash our clothes in addition to our bodies. Tomato patches were also not exempt from these raids. It didn't take a lot to entertain two young (Young) boys.

One country delicacy was a plant that grew wild across the South called pokeweed, commonly referred to as "pokesalid." Pokeweed is poisonous unless cooked properly. Boyd and I knew nothing of this fact. It grows exceptionally well in shaded areas, such as in the shadow of a barn. It could be that it grew well there due to the manure around the barn.

At any rate, Boyd and I were taught to pick the very young, tender leaves and take them to MaMa. She would cook them similarly to how she would cook turnip greens. Yum-Yum!

This meal also had to include pinto beans (dried beans, soaked overnight and then cooked for hours the next day, with a piece of fatback or pork for seasoning), fresh slices of raw, sweet onions, and a large pan of cornbread cooked in a well- seasoned iron skillet.

# 1955 – 1957 Memphis, TN
## (1955 – 1957 1st and 2nd grades)

In 1955, our mother married our stepfather, J.C. Wells. It is possible that they were married in 1954. If so, I simply wasn't aware of it. The first time I remember meeting J.C. was when he and my mother came to our grandparents' house with a little baby girl, my half-sister, Deb.

Boyd and I had no idea that our lives were going to be turned upside down. We had very few clothes between the two of us. Our mother packed our few possessions, and we moved to Memphis, Tennessee. Memphis was a little over one hundred miles from Booneville, and yet, as far as Boyd and I were concerned, it could have been in China or on another planet.

Also, compared to Booneville, Memphis, Tennessee, was bigger than any place that we had ever known. The population of Memphis in 1955 was around 400,000 people.

This is as good a place as any for me to make a couple of comments concerning our new stepfather, J.C. Throughout this book, I make comments concerning J.C. Some of those comments may not be flattering to him. For that, I apologize to J.C. and to his children, my half-sister and half-brother, Deb, and Jay, and to J.C.'s daughters, June and Kay, from his first marriage.

It is not my intention to degrade or defame anyone. I truly loved J.C. like a father most of the time that I knew him. I recognized that he worked his butt off and tolerated some of my mother's shenanigans to see that I had a roof over my head and food in my belly, and for that, I will always be grateful. Between the ages of six and eighteen, I both loved and feared this man.

I never knew and probably will never know what demons possessed J.C.'s existence during most of his life, and I will not judge him poorly for his conduct. The last time I saw and/or talked to J.C. was in the summer of 1979, when I had dinner and visited with him and his new wife near Houston, Mississippi.

I understand that during the final years of his life, J.C. appeared to have made peace with those demons and lived a good life enjoying his wife, my sister Deb and brother Jay. He lived out his life near Belen, New Mexico, and he is buried in the Veterans Cemetery in Santa Fe, New Mexico. I pray that his soul has found peace.

We all need to remember that all of us, and, in my eyes, <u>there are</u> <u>absolutely no exceptions</u>, have our own demons. We must each face and deal with them in our own way. No two people are the same and it's not for any of us to judge others for their conduct.

God Almighty is the true "judge," and my Bible says that His most important commandment is for us to love as we are loved. This does not mean as other men/women love us; it means as our heavenly Father loves us. This is a powerful example and instruction on how to love.

While we are commanded to forgive, we must also remember that we, as individuals, must also pay a price for our sins. We will have to endure the consequences of our actions, good or bad. All relationships are not repairable, and yet, we can move forward and do our best to make amends.

An immense amount of good can come after what may seem like irreparable mistakes.

J.C. Wells

My sister, Deb, and me.

J. C. Wells later in life.

Now that you've heard from "The Reverend" Boyce, also known as "Dr. Sigmund Freud" and the spewing of years of wisdom known as "Boyceology," we'll move on. I do not remember exactly where we lived in Memphis and yet, I was told that it was just a few blocks from Beale Street.

Of course, Beale Street in 1955 was not the Beale Street of today. Elvis was just getting started. In the early 1950's, Beale Street was mostly a mixture of African American "Juke Joints" as well as "the Home of the Blues."

At this time, I don't remember my mom and stepfather going to church, and yet, they would send Boyd and me to church on Sunday mornings. The church was located just a few blocks from our apartment. Boyd and I would walk – back then, our parents didn't worry about us walking alone through the streets of a big city like Memphis.

Of course, I would have to question the mental stability of any unsavory individual who would want to tangle with the two young "Young" boys. As one of my granddaughters would say, to do so, "They would have to be 'cray-cray'!" Mom would give us each a dime to place in the offering plate when it was passed.

I was walking and jumping with my dime in my mouth as young children will do. I swallowed the dime! I was almost certain that, for that sin, I would surely go to Hell. For the next two weeks, I would inspect my stool to retrieve that dime. I never found it.

I wonder if my mom thought, "Why is Boyce, aka, "Pee-Wee" washing his hands so much?" I sure hope that the good Lord has forgiven me for that transgression. I think, given the crap I had to endure for most of my life, that maybe He has. Pun intended!

I started the first grade in Wheeler, Mississippi, and finished the first grade in Memphis.

That's two down, with only twenty remaining.

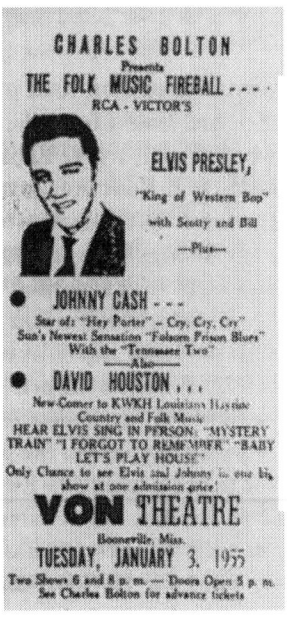

Elvis Presley performed in Booneville, Mississippi before he became an international hit singer and movie star.

# 1957-1958 LITTLE ROCK, AR, DALLAS, TX, & BACK TO MEMPHIS, TN
## (1957 – 1958 2nd and 3rd grades)

J.C. Wells, my stepfather, was sort of a "Jack of all Trades." He was an auto mechanic, a truck driver, and a farmer. He was also a Baptist preacher and an alcoholic. He was most of these things all at the same time, including being a preacher and an alcoholic.

I lived with my mom and J.C. for twelve years minus the one year that I lived in California with my dad and stepmother. To this day, I have never known anyone who knew more about the King James Version of the Holy Bible than J.C.

I only record this to establish a reason (or lack thereof) for my family moving so frequently and to random places.

I do not know what occupation J.C. held while we lived in the cities of Little Rock, Dallas, or Memphis. Most likely, he worked as an automobile mechanic. It's my understanding that he worked as a mechanic in the motor pool during his time in the U.S. Army.

I remember having my first, and I believe, my only birthday party in Little Rock. My birthday and Boyd's were not that far apart (he was born 11/17 and I was born 12/6). Our birthdays were usually celebrated together.

We had a friend in our neighborhood who was also having a birthday. Her parents could afford a party and they very graciously offered to have the two of us join them. We did and, to the best of my memory, we had a blast. I attended the second and third grade or a portion of each in three separate locations.

I remember very little about these schools and have no recollection of my teachers in these years. From time to time, Boyd and I would be taken to Mississippi for a few weeks in the summer to visit our MaMa and PaPa. My mother and J.C. would drive us to their house and come back in a few weeks to pick us up.

For the most part, we visited my mother's family. Occasionally we would visit my dad's people. This is the main reason that I know very little about my dad's side of the family. More than once, we would be living in one location, go to visit our grandparents, only to return home to a totally new home. And, in some, if not most cases, the new house was located in a different state.

This is an assumption, however, I think this occurred in the summer of 1958. Boyd and I were sent to Paden, Mississippi, to spend a few weeks with dad's brother, Coolidge.

Uncle Coolidge was a lot like my dad; he was a very large man, not obese, simply a very tall and large-built man. Uncle Coolidge was always a very jolly man. He laughed often and loudly.

Uncle Coolidge and his wife lived on a small farm on the outskirts of Paden. Paden is located near Tishomingo, Mississippi, only twenty miles from Booneville. Paden is where my family lived just before I was born and where our house burned.

Uncle Coolidge had a small field of corn that he tended using a single mule. For the benefit of those who may not know how one obtains a mule, you simply breed a horse and a donkey, and the resulting colt is a mule. All mules are sterile and have IQ's somewhere on the level of my own. Nevertheless, Boyd and I loved to ride anything that had four legs.

Uncle Coolidge didn't mind so we rode that old mule that summer to the point that the day we left was most likely the happiest day of that mule's life. I digress. Uncle Coolidge had a wooden corn sled approximately six or eight feet long, three feet high, and maybe three feet wide.

The sled was pulled by the mule down the middle of two rows of corn. Uncle Coolidge would guide the mule while Boyd and I would pull ears of corn and throw them into the sled.

When the sled was full, we (I should say that the mule) would drag it to the barn, and Boyd and I would empty the corn into a bin. We would then return to the field and repeat the process until the field was clean.

I never knew why Uncle Coolidge didn't have a wagon with wheels. However, if he had owned one, I wouldn't have had this silly story to tell. I have no earthly idea why this experience was so important to me.

This is basically the only time that I can remember spending any time with any of my dad's family members except for spending a couple of summers with PaPa and MaMa Young. When I say, "spending the summer," I'm basically saying one or two weeks during the summer.

During one of these summer visits to my PaPa and MaMa Young's, Boyd and I enjoyed new adventures. Dad's parents owned a forty-acre farm just a few miles from Paden. PaPa Young farmed using two mules, one white and the other black. I do not know what their names were or even if they had names.

Boyd and I didn't ride these two mules, they were huge. They were, for certain, beasts of burden. PaPa would harness up these two mules and take them down a red clay road to the fields; Boyd and I would follow close behind. When we got to the fields, you couldn't help but notice several medium-sized mounds located throughout the field.

PaPa Young ignored these mounds and would plow and plant right over the top of them. Even though Boyd and I didn't know what caused these mounds, it didn't take long for us to realize that the plow often turned up all sorts of arrow and spear heads as well as an occasional tomahawk head.

We ignored the occasional bone that would appear out of nowhere. It wasn't until much later in my life that I realized these were Native American burial mounds. Apparently, the American Indians buried their dead one on top of the other, along with their most prized possessions.

I suppose they continued this process until the mounds got too high to carry the dirt up the slope. Today, I am sure that disturbing these mounds would not be allowed. During the time that this land was settled by the white man, obviously, no one, except the indigenous people, cared. I kept a collection of arrowheads until it was lost sometime during my stint in the Marine Corps.

This area of Mississippi was rolling red clay hills with the ground gently sloping from the farmhouse, down to the fields and eventually to a swamp and creek. The entire farm was located off a red clay road. The house was located on top of a hill about one hundred yards from the road. There was a steep bank dropping off to the road, and on top of the bank was a huge oak tree.

Some of my most fond memories are of my grandmother Young sitting in an old rocking chair under that oak, telling Boyd and me stories. She could be very funny in her delivery of random stories. Even though my DNA testing indicated that there is very little American Indian in my bloodline, my MaMa Young looked like she had just left the reservation.

She had black hair and very high cheekbones with eyes set back in deep sockets. She claimed to have American Indian blood running through her veins. One day, while sitting under that majestic oak tree, she told us a story of her recollection of the last hanging in Prentiss County, Mississippi.

According to her, this man had "kilt" (that's Mississippi for "killed") his wife. MaMa Young never told us the details of the alleged killing. However, the man was convicted, and as he stood before the judge, he was informed of the jury's decision.

The judge told the man that he had been found guilty of murder and that he was to hang by the neck the following morning at sunrise until he was dead, dead, dead. The judge asked the man if he had any final words for the court. The man said, "Yes! You all can kiss my ass until it's red, red, red!"

According to MaMa, he hung the next morning in front of a huge crowd who had brought picnic baskets full of all sorts of goodies for the big event.

After telling us of this hanging, she almost fell out of her chair laughing. I was never certain if she was being serious or if this was simply an entertaining tale to tell the kids.

One day, a "Billy goat" (a male goat) wandered up to the house when we were staying with our grandparents. We gave him an original name: "Billy." This goat was more like a pet dog than a goat. He followed Boyd and me around the farm, and he seemed to love it when one of us (mostly me) would get on our knees and play head bump with him...that explains a lot, doesn't it?

During that same visit, Boyd and I had found a piece of old rusty sheet metal roofing, and we rolled up one end, attached a rope, and used it as a toboggan. We would slide down the red clay bank between the large oak and the dirt road running in front of the house. On one such adventure, I fell off the sled and cut one of my feet on the metal.

The cut wasn't that bad; however, I had difficulty getting back up that embankment. We solved that problem by tying the rope to Billy, and he helped me get up the hill. Something tells me that this was more about adding drama to the adventure than a necessity.

# The Wells

In the late 1950s or early 1960s, Mr. Wells found a man named "Joseph" hitchhiking on the highway near Vardaman. Mr. Wells offered him a ride to the Wells' family house, a bath, and a hot meal.

I assume that Mr. Wells also offered Joseph a job. Joseph was a very small man, and it was obvious that he was not accustomed to hard farm work. I assume that's also why eventually, he moved into the small room of the house and became their house boy.

Joseph was an awesome cook, and he did all the household chores. He cooked, cleaned, did the laundry, and basically never complained. I'm not sure how long Joseph stayed with Mr. and Mrs. Wells, but I'm certain he stayed until Mr. Wells was killed in 1969. I think the last time that I saw Joseph was at Mr. Wells' funeral.

Joseph was very quiet and almost never spoke unless he was spoken to. He attended Mr. Wells' nightly Bible study and devotion, and he attended church with the Wells. I'm certain that there are numerous other very interesting stories concerning Joseph, however, I'm also sure that none of us will ever know them all.

There was a piano in the Wells' parlor. I don't remember Mrs. Wells ever playing it but J.C.'s two daughters from his first marriage both played.

J.C.'s daughters, June, and Kay, from a previous marriage.

By most standards, Mr. Wells owned a very large farm. I'm not sure of the exact acreage but it was rumored that he had at least 300 acres planted in sweet potatoes alone, cotton, some corn (maize), and very little else. He also always had cows, horses, and pigs.

I can remember helping with castrating the pigs. Boyd and I had the job of catching the pigs one at a time. I cannot understand to this day why, after they witnessed the first castration, the remaining pigs didn't run like Hell or simply drown themselves in the pond.

Once we caught the pigs, J.C. would hold the pig down and Mr. Wells would use a very sharp knife and remove the pig's testicles so fast it would make your head spin.

Next, he would slap a little used axle grease on the mutilated testicle sack and let the pig go. The pig usually ran to the nearest mud hole and slid his butt through it. After about an hour the pig would act like nothing happened. It took me days to get over the trauma of just watching. I walked bowlegged for a week.

It's always been my understanding that Mr. and Mrs. Wells came to Mississippi from Texas many years earlier. As far as I know, all three of their boys were born in Mississippi.

Mr. and Mrs. Wells and their three sons (L to R): Jordan Conrad, Jr. (J.C.), Dunas, and Billy.

During the several times that we lived with or near the Wells' family farm, Boyd and I worked on the farm just like any of the hired hands. The only difference was that Boyd and I did not get paid. I assume that room and board was considered enough pay.

There were eleven families who lived on the Wells' farm. Mr. Wells provided each family with a one room house, a smokehouse, and a small garden plot. These families worked the farm and were paid some small amount other than board and keep.

Mr. Wells also provided rides for all who lived on his farm on every Wednesday to go to the County Courthouse to collect their "commodities." These commodities included basic food items such as flour, corn meal, salt, and pepper as well as cans of Spam and blocks of cheese.

During this time, "welfare" was in the form of commodities rather than money. The families were all white except for one African American man and his wife. They were all related in some form or fashion. They all worshiped Mr. Wells or "Mr. Connered" as they called him. Of course, his full name was Jordan Conrad Wells.

While there was one black family on the property, they lived in a separate part of the farm. I don't know if that was by choice or not. I think at least some of them crossed the fence from time to time. One of the white ladies had a son about my age and it was obvious that his father was black, a huge "no-no" in Mississippi during this time.

The black man's name was "Snooks." It would have been very difficult to not like Snooks. He was extremely hard working and funny. Snooks was responsible, at least in part, for teaching me how to fish, hunt rabbits and squirrels using a single shot 22 caliber rifle and an old beagle with just one ear.

It was rumored that the beagle had lost its ear while fighting a bobcat. If the truth be known, Snooks could have easily shot it off accidentally. Snooks drank a bit.

We were working on the farm picking and sorting sweet potatoes on our hands and knees one Monday morning. There must have been at least 20 of us but Snooks was nowhere to be seen. We looked up to see Mr. Well's truck coming down the dirt field road leaving a cloud of dust behind it.

The truck came to a screeching halt in front of us with Snooks hanging on in the back for dear life. Mr. Wells jumped out of the cab while Snooks was getting out of the bed of the truck. Mr. Wells was swearing like a sailor. He took off his old felt hat and threw it on the ground and started kicking it and saying, "Snooks, why in the Hell do you do this to me? Every Monday morning, I have to go down to the town jail and bail you out!"

Snooks removed his much older felt hat and held it to his chest with both hands, lowered his head and said "Mr. Connered, if you could just be a nigger one Saturday night, you'd never be nuttin' else."

Please know that those were the exact words of Snooks, not anything that I added. Mr. Wells simply shook his head, got back in the truck, and sped off to God only knows; he loved Snooks, but Snooks could and did get under his skin.

The "N" word was commonly used during my younger years, and I had no idea that it was offensive until later in my life. My coming of age, so to speak, from a racial perspective will be shared later.

There was a good side to Mr. Wells however there was also something else that I can only imagine. On several occasions a man would come by the house after dark and talk to Mr. Wells on the front porch.

Mr. Wells would go back to his bedroom and come out with an old pistol wrapped in a newspaper, get in his pickup truck, and drive to places unknown to us. Several hours later he would return, and no one ever asked him any questions.

I can only speculate; this was Mississippi in the 1950's and 1960's. I was told once by J. C. that the KKK didn't just "correct" black people. If a white man ignored his family or beat his wife, the KKK were also responsible for "correcting him."

I didn't know what "correcting him" meant nor did I really want to know. In total, we lived near Vardaman and the Wells' on three separate occasions. Stories of our times there may not be in order. I really can't remember my age or the actual dates of our stays.

Mr. Wells was a devout Christian, went to church every Sunday and to prayer meetings every Wednesday evening, etc. Each evening, prior to bedtime, he led his entire family in reading the Bible and praying. He never ate a meal until grace was said over it. This is a routine that I learned from him and continue to this day.

Skip ahead to one morning in Vietnam, after a particularly difficult two nights of constant bombardment with rockets, mortars and constant "Sapper Attacks" on our security perimeter. [Surprise attacks by elite North Vietnamese Communist units known as "sappers" were one of the most serious—and feared—threats to Americans and the infrastructure of US military bases in Vietnam.]

I was on the radio talking to a counterpart in Da Nang. He asked me if it was true that we were under attack most of the previous two nights. I told him that it was indeed true, and I didn't mind telling him that I don't think that I've ever prayed so hard in my life.

One of my Marine friends standing nearby said to me, "I didn't hear you praying." I simply responded, "That's because I wasn't talking to you." Most likely, I also used a few USMC expletives, but this book is intended to be read by all ages, including young children who I love dearly.

I can honestly say that Mr. Wells taught me to pray. He also taught me that you don't have to be perfect to pray. Thank God for that! His method of prayer was simple: simply talk with God as you would with your own father. The "how" wasn't important.

He would say that fancy words meant nothing to God, only the fact that you wanted to communicate with your Almighty Father.

# THE GRENADA LAKE EVENT

J.C., my mom, my sister Deb, my brother Boyd, and I were on our way from Memphis to visit family in Vardaman, which was home at the time. J.C., as was his normal routine, stopped by a moonshiner's place. I honestly think he knew the exact location of every one of them in the entire state of Mississippi. Before long, he was, at a minimum, two sheets to the wind.

Moonshiners were the norm in Mississippi during these times because Mississippi was a "dry" state, meaning that it was illegal to buy or sell alcohol anywhere in the state. This law was responsible for making many moonshiners very rich people.

It was late at night and very difficult to see even if you were sober, which he wasn't. He turned on a very old, paved road, and we sped through a yellow barricade that said, "CAUTION BARRICADE

AND LAKE AHEAD." The yellow barricade had a kerosene pot at each end to bring attention to the hazard ahead, and they were burning.

As we flew through the barricade and hit a mound of dirt just beyond, we were quickly airborne. I think while we were still airborne, I heard J. C. yell "Bar-a-cade, what the Hell is a bar-a-cade?"

Fortunately for us, the water that we landed in was only 3-4 feet deep. Mom got out of the right front seat with Deb in her arms; J.C. exited the left front seat totally sober, and Boyd and I somehow got out of the back seats. In those days, there were no seat belts in cars.

To this day, I have no idea how we got from that place to our home at least thirty miles away. I am sure that all of us, including J.C. were in shock, not to mention how terribly I soiled my pants.

A kerosene pot used to indicate
a dangerous situation.

Another remembrance: Once in the early 1970s, I drove with my stepmom and sister, Sharon, from Savannah, Georgia to Jacksonville, Florida on old U.S. Highway 17 at night (this was prior to the completion of Interstate 95). It was pouring rain and I never broke 40 miles per hour.

I can't remember why we were going to Jacksonville, however, that was one very scary drive. You couldn't tell where the edge of the pavement ended and where the shoulder began.

A little tidbit that might interest some of the readers of this book: Back in the 1950's, they did not paint lines on the side of highways. I know that this was true in most states in which we lived. If you have
ever driven at night on a black-top paved highway with no painted side lines, then you can surely appreciate the individual who produced that idea.

# THE CHRISTMAS DAY NATCHEZ TRACE

# PARKWAY ADVENTURE

The Natchez Trace Parkway

The distance from Vardaman, Mississippi, to Booneville, Mississippi, is only about 75 miles. One of the most scenic drives anywhere in this country is the 444-mile Natchez Trace Parkway that runs through parts of Tennessee, Alabama, and Mississippi. It's a scenic highway for non-commercial vehicles only and has a maximum speed limit of 45 miles per hour.

We were living in Vardaman and spent Christmas morning with J.C.'s parents. Our plan was to spend Christmas evening and night with our mother's parents in Booneville.

J.C. had borrowed his brother Billy's brand-new Rambler American station wagon. It was two-toned dark blue and baby blue---a genuinely nice automobile. It had snowed the day before, and plenty of ice remained on the roads, especially on the Parkway, which wasn't used much during winter.

Once again, J.C. apparently couldn't make that little drive without visiting the local moonshiner. We were exceeding the posted speed limit by at least 20 mph when we topped a hill and encountered a very long stretch of ice covering the entire road.

J.C. lost control of the automobile, and we began to spin, and just when I thought we were headed toward certain death, the ice stopped, and we hit the dry pavement 90 degrees to our intended direction.

The car flipped on the driver's side and slid for a considerable distance before stopping in the middle of the parkway. I was on the driver's side in the back seat. We all climbed out of the car without a scratch.

Boyd, J.C., and I rocked the car until it finally fell upright on all four wheels. Once again, no seat belts. We had no injuries. The entire left side of the car was totaled, and unless you count the huge brown stain in the exact spot where I had been sitting, there was no damage inside.

SMARTEST, MOST ECONOMICAL STATION WAGON ON THE ROAD

**Rambler**
*Super 4-Door Cross Country for 1958*

After what seemed like hours, J.C. finally got the car started, and we continued along our way, leaving a huge smoke screen behind us to a very Merry Christmas in Booneville, Mississippi. I have no idea how J.C. explained that one to Billy, and thank God, I didn't have to be present.

# POND TORNADOES

I don't know if anyone reading this book will have ever experienced taking a bath in a farm pond. This was a common experience for Boyd and me in Mississippi.

I can think of at least three different ponds at three separate house locations where Boyd and I would take a bath towel (we were civilized, after all), a washcloth, and a bar of soap with us to the pond. The soap was usually homemade lye soap.

These were the same ponds where the livestock drank, pooped, peed, etc. We would play and bathe and didn't think a thing about the fact that the cows and horses also bathed in these ponds. The livestock and we humans also urinated in the same pond.

Isn't Mother Nature a wonderful wastewater treatment facility?

Okay, I'm getting further and further from my intended story. This writing stuff is exhausting; I need a drink.

Most of you probably don't know that after catfish hatch, they stay in a very tight swarm for safety. Apparently, they do this to fool their predators. The predators think that hundreds of baby catfish are one huge creature. When the swarm feels threatened, they start to swim in circles creating what we called a "pond tornado."

I made a grave mistake one day, and I'm telling you this to help you avoid the same mistake the next time you are bathing in a Mississippi pond. I was going to catch a handful of these baby catfish and take them to another pond that I was pretty sure didn't have any catfish.

DO NOT try this with your bare hands. It felt like I had grabbed a red wasp's nest with my hands. I cannot express how much that HURT! It's been said that we learn from every mistake that we make. By now, I should be a genius!

## SAVING BOYD'S LIFE

On one of these bathing trips to the local pond, Boyd and I were swimming and just being boys before we bathed. To better set the stage, I need to tell you how Mississippi farm ponds are constructed. All you must do is find a small creek and build a dam across it. The dirt used for the dam construction is simply dug from the future pond side of the dam and that's it.

You will eventually have a pond with very little effort. This process leaves a relatively deep area near the dam, sometimes referred to as the "borrow pit."

The water gets much more shallow the further you go upstream from the dam. I had learned to swim very early in my young life; Boyd had not.

We were playing in the shallow end of the pond and at one point I swam across the deep water or borrow pit near the dam, this was only a distance of maybe thirty feet. I was on the bank looking for my soap and washcloth when I heard Boyd struggling. He had attempted to follow me.

I have no idea if he thought I had walked across the bottom or maybe he thought he had miraculously learned to swim. I jumped in after him and I honestly thought he was going to kill both of us.

Eventually, he jumped on my shoulders, and I walked under water until he could grab a bush and pull himself onto the dam. I think I added more fertilizer to the pond during that experience.

# RAISING CHICKENS (RHODE ISLAND REDS) AND THE 4-H CLUB

Early in my freshman year of high school in Vardaman, Mississippi, someone talked me into joining the school's 4-H club. 4-H stands for 'Head, Heart, Hands, and Health."

I had no earthly idea what 4-H was or what to expect. And yet, someone convinced me that it was an easy class for an "A," and I was all in. Some anonymous donor gave me 50 Rhode Island Red chicks. They were cute little yellow birds.

No, this is not going to go the way of the kitty-sickles. I got my step-grandfather to donate the corn to feed the chicks and I scraped up some spare chicken wire from somewhere on the farm. I built a large chicken pen with a roof of chicken wire.

The farm attracted all sorts of predators, such as foxes, bobcats, raccoons, and flying raptors (hawks, etc.), not to mention snakes and a very playful sheepdog who happened to love the taste of chickens.

By some incredible stroke of luck, I was able to raise all 50 chicks into adult chickens. I entered four of them in the local county fair livestock show. I'm sure it was one of my first miracles. Of the four chickens that I entered, I took 1st, 2nd, and 3rd place. I was an instant 4-H hero.

What took place next was my second lesson on why one does not get attached to farm animals. The very next day J.C. and my mom killed the entire 50 chickens and put them in Mr. and Mrs. Wells' freezer.

I then understood their kindness by providing me with all that corn. I'll have to admit they did taste very good on Sunday afternoons, any way they were cooked. For the most part, they were crispy fried and delicious.

# MISSISSIPPI MOONSHINE RUN

As I have mentioned before, Mississippi during the 1950s and 1960s was a "dry" state, meaning that the production and/or sale of any beverage containing alcohol was illegal. This was Mississippi's attempt to keep that "evil drink" out of our state and to keep the state safer. I think that all it did was create a flourishing business in moonshining.

It was common in rural Mississippi for twelve- year-old boys to drive most farm equipment, including 2-ton flatbed trucks, pretty much wherever they wanted. One afternoon, J.C. and I were returning from the fields, and I was driving the 2-ton flatbed down a narrow red clay road looking for, you guessed it, a moonshiner's house. We were not really looking, J.C. knew exactly where it was located.

In the backwoods of Mississippi, on red clay country roads, there were bridges crossing most, but not all, creeks. These bridges were nothing more than heavy timbers crossing the creek with 2 X 12 oak boards nailed across the top. The average width of these bridges was maybe eight feet, with room for only one vehicle at a time. There were no side rails, just a flat bridge.

We had gone to several moonshining establishments prior to this one so J.C. was feeling no pain. Isn't it funny how a drunk knows so very much about just about everything? I'm not sure if there was such a thing as a speed limit on these old Mississippi dirt roads but I'm sure that very few people paid much attention to them if there were any.

I was cruising along at what I deemed a reasonable speed when J.C. made an executive decision that my speed wasn't reasonable.

He placed his size 9 Brogan on top of my right foot and pressed the accelerator all the way to the floor and held it there while taking another swig from the fruit jar. The truck would only do about 80 MPH, thank God.

We crossed one of these bridges doing all that the old truck would do, and we narrowly missed a green John Deere tractor pulling a disk harrow approaching the other end of the same bridge.

I'm sure that the driver of the tractor was as scared as I was. I soiled my three- time hand-me-down blue jeans. J.C. never said another thing all the way home. I started to ask J.C. if I could have a swig from his jar. I really needed that swig… and yet, it was another time that God was watching over me.

A working moonshine still from the 1950s.

# 1959-1960
# OKLAHOMA CITY, OK, DALLAS, TX, DURANGO, CO, & MEMPHIS, TN
(1959 – 1960 5th Grade)

A typical irrigation canal in the Midwestern, US.

    We were living not far outside of Oklahoma City. In those days, very wide irrigation canals were common. These canals were used to bring water into farming areas that didn't receive sufficient rainfall during the growing season. These canals were, for the most part, concrete-lined, and most were located near main roads.
    The water was clean and only contained a few snakes, frogs, etc. At least I never saw any horses or cattle bathing in them. These canals made wonderful weekend recreation areas. You could fish and swim in most of them. These canals were deep, maybe ten feet or so. With a great deal of difficulty, you could walk up the concrete banks of the canals.

One afternoon, J.C. and Mom decided to take us boys and our sister for an afternoon at the canal. Deb was too young to swim or even to get near the canal. So, Mom watched Deb on a blanket on the bank while keeping the ants out of our picnic lunch.

J.C. wasn't aware that I could swim so he decided to teach Boyd and me to do so. He took Boyd first, after all, he was the oldest. J.C. threw Boyd as far as he could throw him into the depths. He didn't wait to see how Boyd was doing and he immediately threw me in behind him. I thought it was funny, but Boyd was struggling for his life. The old saying that if you throw someone who doesn't know how to swim into the water then they will learn quickly simply isn't always true.

Fortunately, J.C. was not so drunk that he couldn't swim, so he dove in and saved Boyd. I was so excited that J.C. did so because I'd already had all the fun of being the lifeguard for Boyd. That day, at the canal, Boyd and I probably both would have drowned. I couldn't reach the bottom, and being "Pee-Wee," I'm sure I couldn't have pulled him out.

While living a few miles outside of Dallas, and Dallas wasn't anywhere near the size it is today, we stayed in a very old ranch-style house in the middle of nowhere.

We did have running water inside the house, although it smelled like rotten eggs. The most important luxury we had was a telephone. This was not your ordinary telephone, and it certainly wasn't a cell phone. In fact, it was maybe 12" wide, 12" deep, and 36" high, and it hung on the wall.

It had a mouthpiece on the front and an earpiece on a three feet long cord. It had a 3" handle on the right side, and to call someone, all you had to do was first listen to make sure no one else was on the line. If no one was already talking on the "party line" (meaning multiple homes were connected to the same telephone line), you simply turned the small handle on the right side and a very unfriendly old lady (telephone operator) would say "Number please."

You would tell the lady the number (which was actually a series of letters and numbers, i.e., BR549), and she would connect you. You didn't have any choice because this phone didn't have a dial or numbers for you to use. Women primarily operated these "switchboards."

Another recalled memory of an earlier time in Durango: We lived for a brief time while I was in the third grade, just outside of Durango, Colorado. We lived in an early 20th-century vintage motel.

The motel was located just south of Durango along Highway 160. A railroad track ran parallel to the highway. Across the highway, no more than a few hundred yards away, was a drive-in movie theater.

Boyd, Deb, and I would sit on a stone wall in front of our house and watch the movies from across the highway. We couldn't hear what was being said but what the Hell? It was free.

These "apartments" were simply old, semi-flat roofed motel rooms. Each room included an added sink, stove, and refrigerator. The room's original bathroom already existed (this was a luxury for us, running water and an indoor toilet).

Two sleeping areas were separated by a curtain that could be drawn for "privacy." There was no such thing as a dining area. Most of our meals were eaten either outside or while sitting on the side of the bed. Boyd, Deb, and I slept in the same bed.

The area around our apartment was beautiful. The mountains were behind us as well as beyond the drive-in theater. The Animas River was across the highway. There was also a stockyard just south of the drive-in theater. You could smell it from where we lived.

Boyd and I would put pennies on the railroad tracks and wait for the train to come by. After the train passed, we would find the pennies, and they would be as flat and as thin as a sheet of paper. It doesn't take much to entertain young boys.

The only thing that I can remember concerning the school in Durango was at recess one day, a boy had brought a stamp collection to school. I'm reasonably sure that it belonged to one of his parents.

At any rate, we were on the playground, and it was very windy. He dropped the box that held the collection and stamps went everywhere. All the kids were running around the playground chasing stamps. Isn't that a peculiar memory?

Near our home outside of Durango, Colorado
(L – R), Mr. Jordan Conrad Wells, Sr., Deb, and me.
The drive-in theater screen is in the background,
as well as a mountain named "Moving Mountain"
...I never saw it move.

When we moved from Durango back to Vardaman, the five of us piled into an old, worn-out automobile. I am not sure of the brand or model, but we rarely had a reliable vehicle.

We drove south from Durango and were passing through the panhandle of West Texas when the car broke down. I do not know exactly what broke, but apparently, it was serious.

This happened in an area where you see those signs that say, "Last chance for gas for 100 miles." J.C. walked until he found someone who was willing to send a tow truck to take us to a very old, dilapidated service station. Obviously, we didn't have much money, and like I said, J.C. was a very good mechanic, so he and the station owner struck up a deal.

J.C. would work in the guy's station in trade for the parts for the repairs needed on the car. The only problem was that we were in the middle of nowhere. Where were we going to live while the repairs were being made?

Located behind the gas station was an incredibly old, rusty, and abandoned dirt-track racing car. It had only one seat for the driver and no glass in any of the windows, including the front windshield. It had no tires and was sitting on concrete blocks. The man agreed to let us use that old car as a place to stay while our car was being repaired.

My mother unpacked a few quilts, etc. to spread on the racing car's floor. There was a water spigot located behind the gas station, so we had plenty of water for cooking and bathing. For the most part, we ate saltine crackers and baloney for almost two weeks. Inside the gas station, the man sold some groceries, so we also had sliced white loaf bread. Yum-yum!

Mom's major concerns were the side-winder rattlesnakes, tarantula spiders, and scorpions. During our stay, we saw all three, but fortunately, not in our "home." Boyd and I spent most of our time chasing horned toads and exploring the desert.

A great memory from those days spent in the desert was the nights. There was extraordinarily little light pollution in the desert, and you could see millions and millions of stars. I saw the Milky Way like no other time in my life. The Milky Way looked almost like a thin cloud stretching completely across the sky. It was just another great adventure for a couple of young boys.

In the winter of 1958, we were living in Memphis and attending a Baptist church. I cannot remember the name of the church. However, it was for sure a Baptist church. Mom and J.C. would have thought that any other denomination would have been sacrilegious. The congregation was constructing a new building.

I'm not sure what the new building was going to be used for, but it was going to have a basement. J.C. was helping with the construction and Boyd, and I also helped by mixing mortar and carrying concrete blocks and five-gallon buckets full of mortar to the men who were laying the concrete blocks.

This was exceedingly difficult work for a skinny ten-year-old. We did not have work gloves and our fingers would bleed at night, making us dread having to do it all again the next day.

We were nearing completion of the basement walls when late one night, J.C. received a call from the pastor. There was a serious freeze that night and the red clay on the outside of the basement walls had frozen, swollen, and most of the walls had collapsed.

This news was heartbreaking because we knew that not only would we have to rebuild them, but we'd also have to salvage as many concrete blocks as possible. Carrying new concrete blocks was one thing. Salvaging the ones that we could was back-breaking work, not to mention our poor damaged fingers. We eventually finished the basement.

During the following summer, this church was under the pastoral leadership of Brother Lamon, I can't remember, or possibly I never knew, his first name. Brother Lamon held an old-fashioned summer revival.

If you've never attended one of these, it can be quite the spectacle. The church didn't have air conditioning, although it did have cardboard "funeral fans" spread out over all the pews.

These fans were called funeral fans because the local funeral home provided them in volume, free of charge to all churches. Of course, the funeral home's name, address, and phone number was clearly displayed on one side of the fan, the other side usually featured an artist's rendering of Jesus. What better place was there to advertise?

There was this elderly (maybe 30–40-year-old) lady who attended the revival services every evening. She would get caught up in the Holy Spirit and start running up and down the aisle, waving her hands in the air and screaming at the top of her lungs "Praise Jesus!"

I was ten years old and that lady scared Satan out of me. I was certain that she was a witch. (That makes two witches in my life by this time...there would be others.) I had this thing about witches.

At any rate, I fell under conviction for several days. I was horrified that I was going straight to Hell. Given all the adventures I'd had (some might call it the "trouble that I had gotten into"), I was certain that I needed salvation.

One night, while we were having the benediction, a short or not so short period of time after the preaching, which was an opportunity afforded to anyone in the congregation to come forward and be saved. That meant getting saved from going to Hell.

When Brother Lamon asked everyone to bow their heads, no one was looking around, every eye was
closed, he would say a prayer for all the lost sinners in attendance.

I did as I was instructed, and I prayed to God, saying, "Dear God, I am too scared to move from the center of this pew and walk down that long aisle, and, by the way, that screaming old lady can't be far away." I was terrified.

I prayed that if God would send someone to take me by the hand, I'd go forward. Brother Lamon had not asked for anyone needing salvation to raise their hand, so I know that didn't give me away.

However, at one point in his prayer, I opened my eyes and "lo and behold"… that's Southern-speak for "Good God Almighty," Brother Lamon was standing right next to me with his hand reaching for my hand.

He said, "Son, do you need to do something? "I said, "Why yes, I think I do." We walked hand-in-hand down the aisle to the altar, (I also had one eye looking for that witch), and once there, I dropped to my knees, and I asked Jesus to take control of my life.

I honestly believe that I received Jesus Christ into my heart at that altar, and I started developing a lifelong relationship with Him that night. Over the years, I've had time to ponder that night.

I can say that my life changed, my sinning didn't stop instantly or entirely, and I've doubted salvation many times since. The one thing that makes me cling to my Christian beliefs is that, at an incredibly early age, it became obvious to me that if I solely relied on my own abilities to earn salvation, then I was doomed for Hell. The belief that I can obtain salvation through Christ is extremely comforting.

I was baptized shortly after this, and while I really tried to live better, I know that I did not always succeed. For the benefit of those who do not understand baptism, in the Baptist church, it requires getting into a body of water, a tank, a pond, a river, the ocean, any body of water if it's deep enough to completely submerge the one being baptized.

The actual submersion represents the death, burial, and resurrection of Jesus. While baptism isn't required for salvation, the act publicly identifies the one being baptized as a follower of Christ.

Religion and politics are two subjects about which I have always been reluctant to enter into conversations. I suppose it's because I'm simply not qualified in either.

I have strong beliefs in both; however, I'm not schooled sufficiently in either to pursue debates. I will say that I have a strong Christian faith, as well as strong conservative opinions.

I do believe that any politician of any party affiliation who isn't willing to compromise is a dangerous individual. Compromise is what makes us civil. One must remember that our great country, our world, is made up of a vast variety of people. One fix does not work for everyone.

Darn, now I've become a preacher and a politician! Glory be! As the old preacher would say, "Can I get an 'Amen'?"

# 1960-1961 MEMPHIS, TN & WEST MEMPHIS, AR
### (1960 – 1961 6th Grade)

During my childhood, we had two close encounters with tornadoes. The first one occurred when we lived outside the city of West Memphis, Arkansas. We lived in a house located on what was once a dairy farm.

The house had a basement that was only about 3-4 feet in height. It was easy for Boyd, Deb, and me to get in, but it was a tad more difficult for the adults.

We had been experiencing bad storms so my mom decided that we should all go to the basement. The only access was via a slightly sloped door on the outside of the house. The door was built of heavy timbers and could be locked from the inside. We lay on the bare ground, and the storm got so extreme that we had to place our hands over our ears.

We heard this huge scream, or so it seemed, that turned out to be the house moving about three feet off its foundation. We had to move a few feet to keep from getting wet, but we spent the entire night in that basement. Once the sun came up, we crawled out from under the house to inspect the damage.

Several buildings near our house were destroyed, they were simply gone; not a thing was left. The house that we were under was intact for all intents and purposes, although it had slid askew to its foundation. Boyd and I had two bikes that we had pieced together from several old, discarded bikes, and they both were gone.

We later found both, about a quarter of a mile away, near the top of an old oak tree. They were not repairable. It would have been one Hell of a ride if we could have ridden them that evening.

While living in the garage apartment in Memphis, we had our second encounter with Mother Nature. The block that we lived on was filled with large, beautiful old homes. Most of the old homes had garage apartments that were accessed via an unpaved lane. We lived in one such garage apartment.

One night, a tornado passed through our neighborhood. We had no prior notice of such storms as we do today other than a very annoying siren that blasted only after the storm had passed. Our apartment faced due North toward the big house directly in front of us. We parked on the East side of our apartment off the unpaved lane.

The apartment to our West was only about ten feet or so from our western wall. The tornado came through late at night, and my mom had gathered up all of us kids. We all took shelter in the bathroom, which was located under a stairwell in the center of the house. Instinctively, I think that she knew that something terrible was about to happen.

The storm came through like a roaring lion. I don't know why everyone says that tornadoes sound like a locomotive train. I've now experienced four and, to me, they all sounded like you're standing behind a Boeing 747 jet.

The storm didn't even remove a single shingle from our house while the building immediately to our West was completely gone except for the slab. That must have been some DACBFM luck at work.

There was a vacant lot a short distance down the alley. The lot was grown up with weeds that were about knee high. I was twelve years old and still very much into playing cowboys and Indians. To be politically-correct I should call it those evil cattle-herding villains and the indigenous people of the western hemisphere.

I played an Indian, as I always did like to be the underdog, and, to avoid those awful cowpokes, I dove into the tall grass, and directly onto a broken coke bottle. Those villainous cowpokes got me, my left hand still bears the scar of the resulting cut and six stitches. This was one of the few times that I ever went to the hospital emergency room.

Not long after the infamous cowboy encounter, a man knocked on our door, it was my dad. He had just returned from one of three, two-year Germany assignments for the US Army. I had seen my dad's picture, which my mom kept displayed somewhere in the house.

I'm not sure how J.C. dealt with that. I had not seen my dad since I was old enough to remember. I did recognize him, but only from the picture. His wife, Agnes, was living in Newport, Arkansas with her two children, Sharon, and Billie Steve Wilson. Dad wanted Boyd and me to spend a couple of weeks with them in Newport before he went on his stateside assignment.

My mom agreed. So, Boyd and I packed a small bag and went with dad, a perfect stranger, to a place where we had never been, to another perfect stranger and her two children whom we had never met to spend the next two weeks. What was so different about that? We were accustomed to going places where we had never been and meeting complete strangers.

I met Sharon, my beloved sister, and Melvin, her soon to be husband, while on this little vacation. Sharon and Melvin were married during this visit. The first time that I met Melvin, he was the typical early sixties teenager, complete with rolled up blue jeans, white tee shirt with a pack of Lucky Strikes rolled up in one sleeve, a huge western belt buckle, and a flat-top haircut.

Sharon was a cute, dark haired, bubbly teenage girl who was smitten with Mel. Billie Steve was very similar to Mel, only cooler in my simple mind. After all, Billie Steve was closer to my age.

Billie and I hit it off quickly and even though Billie wasn't old enough to legally drive, he and I went riding one afternoon. I assume that he had permission to use the car. We went to the local Dairy Queen (DQ).

The girls who worked at the DQ came to your car to take and deliver your orders. They were all on roller skates. Again, you can't make this crap up! Billie Steve had a talent for talking and sounding just like Donald Duck.

When a waitress came to his window to take our order, Billie Steve said, "Hello Baby" in his Donald Duck voice. The poor girl was laughing so hard that she fell flat on her butt!

I have never mastered that talent, but I have tried it with varying results. This was my first ever visit to a drive-in restaurant. I ordered a "Frito-Chili Pie" and a coke. I still "love me some Frito-Chili Pie!"

A typical Dairy Queen roller skating waitress in the early 1960s.

Before we had to go back to Memphis, one day we all went to a swimming area on the White River. Everyone was swimming, splashing, and having a grand old time, except for me.

That stupid encounter with the evil cowboys back in the frontier of Memphis left me with strict instructions not to get near a swimming hole until my hand was completely healed, it wasn't. Those damn cowboys won again!

This was a very enjoyable vacation for Boyd and me. We started relationships that we would maintain to some level for the remainder of our lives, some stronger than others, and that was mostly due to geography.

Boyd spent most of his adult life in the Seattle, Washington area, near Billie Steve and I spent most of mine living near Sharon. Living near Sharon included coast-to-coast locations, from Cotati, California to Savannah, Georgia.

# 1961-1962 MEMPHIS, TN & VARDAMAN, MS
### (1961 – 1962 7th Grade)

This time in my life is a little vague. I do remember living in a somewhat nice house not far from Memphis. The nearest town to us was Cordova, Tennessee.

Now I do not know all of the details of this story, but I do have theories. One Friday night, J.C. and my mom decided to take the entire family to a drive-in theater.

Generally, when we did this, in order to escape from paying for two more screaming children, Boyd and I would usually climb in the trunk. Once we were safely inside the theater, we would get out and sit in the back seat or on the hood of the car. One more great adventure for young boys.

On this trip, we did not ride in the trunk. The trunk was full of most, if not all, of the clothes we owned. Once we were in the drive-in theater, we all sat on the ground near the front and near the playground.

J.C. disappeared for most of the movie. Later, on our return trip and when we were almost home, we could see lights from fire trucks and police cars in the distance. When we pulled into the driveway all that was left of the house was the brick chimney. Also, one old car parked next to the house was destroyed.

I never found out what happened that night, but I can only imagine. By the way, that was the only home that J.C. ever owned or, I should probably say the bank owned and it was insured.

It was significantly interesting and very fortunate that we had ALL of our clothes in the trunk, or we would have lost everything.

We had a very pretty and loving Collie named, what else? Lassie. Lassie was obviously scared out of her wits, but we loaded her up and we all went to stay with an aunt in Memphis.

The only place they had for Lassie to stay was in an old shed with a dirt floor located in the backyard. Lassie was confused and scared and not used to being locked up at night.

On one of the nights during our stay, Lassie dug out of the shed and simply disappeared. Cordova was only about thirty miles from where my aunt lived but to me that was a long way.

After two or three days we received a call from one of our neighbors in Cordova asking us to come get our dog. I had no idea how, but she found her way back to the nearest house to ours that burnt. We were able to find someone in Mississippi who wanted Lassie, so she found a new home.

We moved from my aunt's place back to Vardaman, Mississippi and lived in a small unpainted house not far from Mr. and Mrs. Wells. Boyd and I attended school in Houston, Mississippi, about ten miles from where we lived.

One day, J.C. loaded Boyd and me up and we drove to the airport in Houston. Apparently one of J.C.'s childhood friends owned an airplane and he had volunteered to give us a ride.

To that point, it was the most awesome day of my life. Boyd and I sat in the back seat and J.C. rode up front. Boyd and I talked about everything we could see.

I remember arguing with Boyd that, from this high, I was certain you could see an enemy submarine under the water. I think from that day on I was hooked on flying and knew that someday and somehow, I was going to learn how to fly an airplane.

In the mid 1970's, I got my pilot's license. I still fly and own two airplanes to this date although I am selling my beloved Cessna in the summer of 2023 to an international business owner who has an industrial plant in Metter, GA. It will be a sad day and yet, that Cessna and I have had many, many great experiences together.

Me and one
of my favorite hobbies
November 2021

METTER MUNICIPAL AIRPORT
ELEV. 197     FREQ 123.0

When we were growing up, Boyd lived in his own world, far away from the day-to-day issues that kids in our situation had to bear. Boyd's moods would change in an instant and apparently without cause. One moment he'd be totally involved in whatever we were doing and the next, you could tell that he was in his "safe place." I often envied him; I never could master that talent.

This mood-changing was also a source of conflict. Most people, who Boyd and I knew, never understood Boyd, or worse, they misinterpreted his actions as aggression and so they acted accordingly, especially the bullies on campus; and there were always bullies. Usually if you fought one of us, you'd fight both of us if the other was nearby.

Boyd was never afraid of a fight; however, he'd lose interest sometimes and simply stop in the middle of it and walk away. The bullies wouldn't go after him when they had me on the ground. Boyd was a lot bigger than me. This was not a one-time deal; it happened more times than I care to remember.

Boyd was a gentle giant; he couldn't stand the thought of hurting someone. I believe that at some point in the fights, he thought he was close to seriously hurting someone and simply went to his happy place and walked away.

Wouldn't life be so much more pleasant if we all could do that? I could never enjoy that tranquility, I'd stay until someone was seriously bleeding or until someone stopped the fight.

Another random memory: My third-grade class went on a field trip to the local fire station in Houston (MS). We didn't get to ride in a fire truck, but they did give each of us a cheap red plastic fire hat. I kept that hat for years until it got lost somewhere on one of our frequent moves.

# 1962-1963 VARDAMAN, MS & MEMPHIS, TN
## (1962 -1963 8th Grade)

In September 1962, while in the 8th grade in Vardaman, my appendix ruptured. The issue with my appendix had been going on for a couple of years. I would have severe pains in my side/stomach.

J.C. was certain that it was all faked in order to get attention or have things my way. I couldn't convince my mom or stepdad that there was something serious going on. We also very rarely went to a doctor or dentist.

The attacks would come on suddenly and after a day or so they would subside. The best way that I can explain the pain is that it was like a little fellow inside of me trying to cut his way out with a butcher knife.

During this time, I learned a skill that would serve me well for the rest of my life. If I laid perfectly still and focused intently on the pain, I could make it go away. If someone disturbed me during this deep meditation, the pain would return.

I would lie on the floor in a fetal position when doing this. Once, J.C. made me get up and go outside with the other kids and stop "faking" the sickness. I got up, was bent over at the waist, and hobbled outside

Once there, I found a place in the grass, laid down and started the meditation all over again. I will never understand why I didn't die during this time; I had never heard of anyone having re-occurring appendicitis attacks without the appendix rupturing. Once again, more evidence that God had more for me to learn on this side of eternity.

Then, my appendix finally ruptured. All my learned meditation skills wouldn't make the pain go away. My mom finally took me to the local clinic in Vardaman. This clinic had two hospital beds separated only by a curtain.

The clinic was housed in the same building as the fire station and police department. To the best of my knowledge, the clinic had only one doctor, Dr. Calhoun.

Dr. Calhoun must have been related to J.C. because he also loved his moonshine. A couple of years later, the good doctor was killed in a single car accident when he was driving while intoxicated.

I still have a vivid memory of Dr. Calhoun mashing my stomach a few times and saying, "We've got to get this boy's appendix out immediately." They rushed me into the small operating room and gave me a spinal tap.

I would later learn that the proper name for this procedure was a "Lumbar Puncture." I was awake during the entire procedure and was infatuated with the nurse who was wiping the sweat off my face.

I could hear the doctor talking to the nurse about having to take the appendix out in several pieces. They finished, sewed me up and put me in a bed with a metal harness or frame holding my head in a very uncomfortable position. I had to stay in the hospital/clinic with that traction contraption on for three days.

Have you ever tried to read a book, while flat on your back, holding it in front of you? I was later informed that the traction was the procedure they did to prevent paralysis after a spinal tap. I was also told that they were not supposed to give a spinal tap to a minor.

It really didn't matter to me; I survived, had a great scar to show the girls and never had those pains again.

I never lost that ability to make pain go away using only my mind. I do not know what the human mind can accomplish, and yet, I do think that we only use a very small portion of our mind's capability.

A few weeks later, I was helping Mr. Wells load some bags of cattle feed in the back of his truck. Mr. Wells wasn't looking, and he closed the tailgate on my right thumb.

At first, I didn't think it was broken and I was sure that it would be fine in a few days. It wasn't fine; the thumb swelled to twice its normal size and throbbed with pain.

Once again, I went to Dr. Calhoun on my way to school. He remembered me from my three-day stay just a few weeks earlier. He looked at the thumb, rubbed it and left the room.

He came back in with two butcher knives. Rubbing them together, he calmly said, "I think we're going to have to remove the thumb." I think I may have wet my pants. Again, I was good at that.

After he and the nurse had a good laugh over that, he grabbed a scalpel, held my hand very tightly and lanced the thumb, no pain killer. After what seemed like a half gallon of blood and puss came out of the thumb, he put a bandage on it, and I was off to school.

I never had any other issues with it.

# 1963-1964 VARDAMAN, MS & HUGHES, AR
## (1963-1964 9th Grade)

One spring day, a classmate asked me if I was going to play football. I had no idea that football was even played in school. I was completely ignorant of high school sports of any kind. I was near the end of my 8th grade so the only thing I could do was participate in spring practice...I thought, "Why not?"

I enjoyed the practice games and decided to go out for the team during my freshman year. I made the team as a freshman. The following season we had an awful team. One game we played, we could only dress out 13 players.

If you sat on the bench, you had to be one of the absolute worst players in football history. Most of us played both ways, meaning both offense and defense. I played wide receiver on offense and linebacker on defense. I was lucky if I weighed 120 pounds.

We had a wonderful season...we scored only once all year. We played Booneville for our first game of the year and tied their team 7-7. You had ties in high school football back then.

We never scored another point all year. At one point, we were asked by our high school's football association if we wanted to simply drop out. The team voted 13-0 to hang in there for the rest of the season. I think the worst we ever lost was 72 to 0. Damn, we had a good defensive team!

Coach Thomas, our head coach, asked me to go up in the attic of the gym to find some practice equipment. While in the attic, over against the wall, I noticed that there were about two dozen "real" football helmets.

They were all leather, no face mask and they looked like you'd have to be a real man to play wearing that helmet. What I wouldn't give for a few of those now; they are probably worth a fortune.

Although we had plastic helmets, face masks and mouth pieces were not required and the few who chose to wear them were called "sissies." The only face mask available had a single bar, no cages, etc.

Friday, November 22, 1963, is a date that few who were old enough, will ever forget. This date brought shame, confusion, and sadness into my life like I had never experienced to this point.

I was in Mrs. Thomas' freshman English class. Mrs. Thomas was Coach Thomas's wife. Someone came into our classroom and whispered something into Mrs. Thomas' ear. She started to cry and made the announcement that someone had just assassinated President John Fitzgerald Kennedy.

What came next was the thing that confused and shamed me. Most of the class stood up and started applauding and screaming, "That son-of-a-bitch is dead!" I like to believe that the students' reaction to President Kennedy's murder was simply them reflecting their parents' attitudes.

President Kennedy was the first American President to be a Catholic and Mississippi was predominantly protestant. Most people in Mississippi during this time perceived Catholics to be idol worshipers.

Ignorance is a deadly disease in and of itself. I didn't know a lot about politics back then and I probably don't know enough now. And yet, I did know enough about common decency to know that you didn't celebrate the intentional murder of a U.S. President. School was canceled for the day, and everyone went home.

The taking of anyone's life is a serious thing, even in times of war. Life is a precious gift from God and it's not for us as mere mortals to decide when and where someone is to die. If I had only one prayer that I was assured would come to fruition, it'd be that no man, under any circumstances, would ever take another human's life. This is the one and only reason that I've not encouraged any of my children to become a part of any branch of the military.

There is no honor in war, only shame. If the security of my nation was at stake, then I'd be first in line to fight and even die, willingly, to prevent harm to others, and yet, never again will I support war for the sake of war.

I love my country, but I'll never again say "My country, right or wrong." That's exactly what brought Hitler and the Nazi party into power in the 1930's. For some of you readers who may not be familiar with the politics of the early 20$^{th}$ century, please take the time to study and absorb that philosophy from all sides.

Political parties who are not willing to compromise and look at all perspectives are not worth being associated with. This country, for that matter, this world, is made up of an extreme diversity of people, religions, and races.

It is impossible to have what seems right for one to be right for all. Compromise is what makes us civil. Without it, we're doomed. Now, I'll get away from politics and get back to the story.

An interesting story that must be told is about one of the houses that we lived in during this time in my life.

It was a simple four room "shot gun" style house with a hall running the entire length of the house. Each end of that hall was screened with a screen door opening to a covered porch. In the center of the hall was a well where we drew all of our water.

On one side of the hall were two bedrooms. J.C. and mom had the larger of the two, which also had a fireplace. Boyd and I shared the other and shared the same bed. On the other side of the hall was the living room, which also had a fireplace, and the kitchen. Deb and Jay slept in the living room.

Since our bedroom had no source of heat, Boyd and I would place bricks in the fireplace in the living room. After they were sufficiently heated, we would take them out and wrap them in newspaper. Next, we would place them underneath our bed's sheets and quilts that MaMa had made from our worn-out shirts. This would warm up the bed before bedtime. Once the bricks cooled, we would kick them out of bed.

The interior walls of this house were not finished. This means that all of the studs were exposed, and, in some places, you could actually see through cracks to the stars outside. Boyd and I would make our own glue by mixing flour and water and then we would paste newspaper over these cracks to keep the cold and the wind out.

This is the same house where we lived when I raised my blue-ribbon Rhode Island Red chickens. There was an old one car garage behind the house near a small pond. The garage was desperately in need of repairs and was braced on one side to prevent it from tipping over.

While our parents were gone one day, Boyd and I were given specific orders to clean up around the property. We had developed a considerable sized pile of trash that needed to be burned.

We set fire to the pile, which was close to the old garage and I'm sure Boyd and I got sidetracked. Nevertheless, the fire got a little out of control and made its way to the garage. We spotted it in time to create a two-man bucket brigade from the small pond to the garage.

The entire backside of the garage was charred and the two of us looked like we were of African descent, however, we did save the building. Had the fire gone much further, it's unlikely that we would have been able to save the garage or the main house.

We were lucky that day and with the fire contained to the rear of the garage I don't think that our parents were ever aware of the near tragedy.

Most old farmhouses had an outhouse, or a privy. For some unknown reason, this house did not have one. Like all good poor Mississippi farmers, we improvised. J.C. took an old wooden straight-back chair, constructed a seat with a hole in it and placed it in the woods a few hundred feet from the house. When the pile got too high, you simply moved the chair a few feet away and started piling it up again.

Once again, you simply can't make this <u>crap</u> up! This entire operation had to be moved further away in the winter when the leaves fell. After all, we had to maintain our modesty. You had to take the number of pages from the Sears catalog that you thought you would require with you when you had to make a visit to our little "relief station."

If you forgot the catalog pages, or ran out, you'd have to use tree leaves. Have you ever heard of chiggers or red bugs? They are tiny, nasty little blood-sucking bugs that live in the woods and itch like the devil once they bore into your skin. You really don't want them on your butt.

The larger pond was only a few hundred yards from our toilet and that's where Boyd and I enjoyed our weekly baths; take a dump, then take a bath. Life simply doesn't get any better.

Once, during a summer rainstorm, Boyd and I manufactured two boats from scrap wood and enjoyed simple boat races down the roadside ditches. We were bare-footed and wearing only shorts. Life was very simple, not good, but simple.

We had a garden that was located across the dirt road and on an old home-site. The house had long been removed, burned or maybe it simply rotted away.

One summer day, Boyd and I were in the garden hoeing, when one of us hit something metal. We both dove for the treasure. Boyd got to it first; it was an 1899 silver dollar. I'm sure that Boyd kept it all his life and I hope that Boyd's family in Washington state knows where it is today.

Note: "Hoeing" is the process of removing weeds from a crop or garden with a hoe, not an act of prostitution.

I do hate to reflect on the difficult chapters of my life. However, a complete story cannot be told without laying one's soul bare. As previously stated, there were times when I'd go into deep depression. For the life of me, I can't imagine why.

On one such occasion, I was home alone, and, for some unknown reason, I went into one of those dark places where our soul simply doesn't want to go. I went into the kitchen and grabbed the largest butcher knife that I could find.

Then I went to the screened porch and got down on my knees. I pointed the knife to my heart, rocked back and forth, weeping uncontrollably, trying to work up the courage to plunge the knife deep into my chest.

I truly believe the only reason that I was unsuccessful was that I was certain that J.C. would beat the shit out of me had I gone through with it.

I say that tongue-in-cheek, however, that's the way this DACBFM rationalized things during those times. There are times when it pays to be stupid.

Boyd and I dealt with our circumstances in different ways. Boyd sort of went into a fantasy world for protection; I calloused my heart to protect it from our reality. My editor would say that's when a piece of my soul would depart to a "safe place." I suppose you could say that I scared the Hell out of my soul, or maybe my soul was trying to scare me out of my personal Hell.

I don't think either Boyd nor I completely separated ourselves from these efforts in our adult lives. There were times when I would envy Boyd. He would sit under a tree for hours, alone and it was obvious that his body was there and yet, his "inner being" was somewhere far, far away.

I often tried to understand Boyd's personal journey to deal with the stress of our lives and yet, I never asked him where he went during these times. It seemed like it was a very personal subject, and I am not sure that he could have explained it, had I asked.

The closest that I ever came to that deep "escape" was when I would go into deep meditation to make pain go away. I enjoy meditation to this day. Now, it is more for the comfort of my soul.

Sometimes, in telling my story, it appears that I ignore my half-sister, Deb and half-brother, Jay. That is not my intent. They came along years after Boyd and I spent time with our grandparents.

Growing up, after we left our grandparents' home, we never considered Deb and Jay as being half-siblings, they were simply our younger sister and brother.

There is no doubt that their lives were just as difficult and wrought with the same issues as Boyd and mine. All four of us took different paths in life and, by the grace of God, we all survived.

We lost Boyd on August 19, 2004, from a disease that was the direct result of his contact with a defoliant, Agent Orange, while serving a tour of duty with the U.S. Army in Vietnam in 1966. Some soldiers die in combat immediately, while for others, it takes many years. In Boyd's case, it took thirty-eight years, but rest assured, that war killed him.

Maybe where he is now is the same place that he used to go on his journeys sitting under that tree.

I'm certain that he is enjoying peace and enjoying it with his wife, Lynda, and dear son Kenny.

Kenny passed away much too young from a cancer that I am convinced was passed on from his father, again from the result of exposure to Agent Orange.

I believe that the story of Deb and Jay's lives is a book in and of itself. I don't think I'm remotely qualified to tell that story, nor would I attempt to do so.

Nearing the end of 1963 during the month of October, when I was fourteen, an event occurred that will forever remain in the minds of those who are old enough to remember. It was the "Cuban Missile Crisis."

The U.S. had recently moved missiles into Italy and Turkey that could carry nuclear warheads to any target in Europe, including anywhere in the Soviet Union as well as Russia, in just a matter of minutes. In response to this, the Soviet Union started constructing missile launching sites in Cuba, only ninety miles from the southern coast of Florida.

The U.S. intervened and set up a naval blockade around Cuba and stopped Soviet ships loaded with missiles. This crisis only lasted for a little over a month, however, it's probably the closest the world has ever come to an all-out nuclear war.

You must remember that all of this was happening only seventeen years after Germany had surrendered during WWII and the U.S. had dropped the first two atomic bombs in Hiroshima and Nagasaki, Japan.

I have a few dominant memories from this time. We would gather around a black and white TV and watch every move made by either the U.S. or the Soviet Union. We truly expected missiles to start falling out of the sky any minute.

We were taught in school that if we heard a warning siren that we should take shelter under our desks, in hallways, in basements and cover our heads with books...seriously??

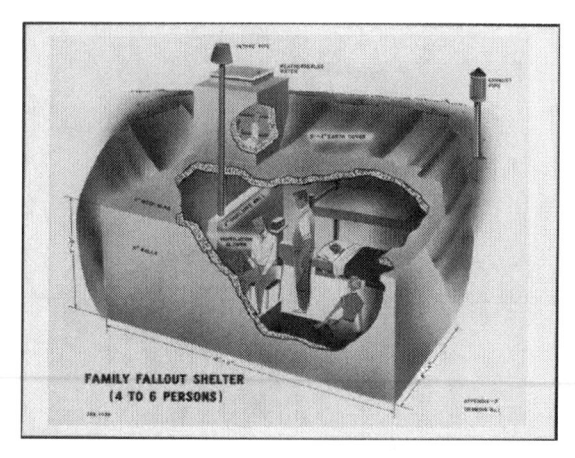

As will always happen during any disaster or crisis, there will be entrepreneurs who want to profit from the situation and capitalize on public fear. Prefabricated bomb shelter sales lots started popping up everywhere.

In Memphis, you could find them on almost every block on what was once a used car lot. You could walk or crawl into a displayed shelter located on the lot, pick out the one you felt best met your family's needs, sign on the dotted line and have one installed on your property for easy monthly payments, once again...seriously??

If the worst should come true, how are all of those dead people going to make those easy monthly payments? To whom are they going to make those payments? You can still see some of these shelters in backyards of older houses today. Our family would visit these bomb shelter lots and window-shop.

However, we could never have afforded such a luxury. Most, if not all, of the shelters were much better built than the houses in which we lived. It was my opinion at the time, that should the worst come to worst, I would prefer that the first nuclear missile simply hit me in the back of the head, problem solved.

In early 1964, near the end of my freshman year of high school, we moved from Vardaman, Mississippi to Hughes, Arkansas. Hughes is an exceedingly small town, I'm not sure that you could even call it a town. Hughes is in the eastern part of Arkansas, about thirty-five miles west, southwest of Memphis, Tennessee. As the crow flies, it's only about fifteen miles west of the Mississippi River.

Hughes is located in flat farming land. Cotton and, in some of the more southern areas, rice were the predominant crops. J.C. took a job on a large farm, with many tractors, trucks, and other farm equipment.

Being a man of many talents, J.C. was a very good mechanic, and he was hired at $90 a week. That was the most that he had ever been paid in his life. The farm also provided him with a nice white frame farmhouse with a picket fence around the yard. The house still exists today and is located between the large plantation house and the huge equipment maintenance garage, referred to as the "shop." There were always tractors, combines, trucks, etc. parked outside the shop waiting their turn to go inside for repairs.

The house we were provided wasn't large and yet, it was larger than most in which we had lived. It did not have air conditioning, and yet, it did have running water and it was heated by a radiator in each room. I have no idea where the radiators got the steam to operate.

One of the reasons that the radiators are important to this story is that one of the major packaged cereal brands of this time was offering a cheap transistor radio for five box tops and $0.50. These radios were AM only and they came with a single earphone as the only means of listening.

The power for these radios was (read closely because you can't make this crap up) derived from the minute electrical charge that is naturally produced in radiators and the metal piping bringing the steam to the radiator. I saved my money and cereal box tops and mailed in my order for the radio.

Amazingly, this radio actually worked! The biggest thing to ever hit the airways in those days was music by the Beatles. I spent hours upon hours listening to songs by the Beatles on that 50-cent radio with a single earpiece.

"I want to hold your hand" was my favorite Beatles tune. I had to lay on the floor near the radiator due to the roughly two-foot-long cord. At the end of the cord with a single gator clip that was attached to the piping of the radiator.

My parents bought a custom 1958 Cadillac convertible (and I have no idea how). It was all white on the outside and had white and red "tuck and roll" interior. It was beautiful.

As indicated earlier, law enforcement officials paid little attention to underage teenagers driving in those days.

After church one Sunday, we had a family come to our house for dinner. This family brought their daughter (no, this story is not going there). After dinner, J.C. suggested that I take this girl to Horseshoe Lake. This was a beautiful lake maybe 6-8 miles east of Hughes.

I can't remember anything about the girl except that she had blonde hair and loved riding in that Cadillac convertible. I don't think I broke 35 MPH all the way there and back. I didn't get my first kiss on that "date," and I don't think I even tried.

The entire trip was totally uneventful. However, I felt that the car and the event were book worthy. I do know that if I could have that girl or that car today, I would take the car, hands down!

One day, J.C. took Boyd and me fishing in Horseshoe Lake. It was one of the only two or three times that I recall J.C. taking us fishing. I don't know where J.C. got the boat, it certainly wasn't ours so it must have been borrowed.

It was a 12-14-foot-long aluminum boat with a motor. The lake is named "Horseshoe" for a good reason. It is long and narrow and is shaped just like a horseshoe.

I think that it was once a spin-off from the Mississippi River or a bayou. In the South, a bayou is what was once a river or tributary that each end had closed in by natural causes. The resulting body of water is called a "bayou."

I don't know what we did right that day, and yet, we all had two fishing poles each. We would row to one end of the lake against the wind and let the wind carry us back to the other end.

We caught brim as fast as we could bait the hooks and put them back into the water. The only reason that we stopped was we ran out of bait.

That was the most fun that I can remember ever having with J.C. and Boyd. I thought that we were finally on a course to a decent life after all the other attempts. That simply didn't happen.

On another day, just a few days before the end of my freshman school year, I was sitting in study hall (in our case this was the old gym with only a half basketball court). I don't think that it was used for its original purpose anymore.

A very tall, dark-haired man walked into the class and spoke to the teacher. For some unknown reason, I knew that the man was my dad.

The teacher called me up front and handed me a written excuse to get out of school for the rest of the day. Dad had asked my mom if he could spend the afternoon with me.

He had decided to take me fishing on the Midway Lake near the Mississippi River. I don't know why it was just me and not Boyd as well except Boyd had dropped out of school and was most likely working... that's just the way it was.

Dad and I fished all afternoon and caught nothing. On the way home, he informed me that he was returning from Germany and was going to be stationed in California.

He asked if I'd be interested in spending the summer with him at his new duty station and I said, "Absolutely, I would."

It took a little sweet-talking to convince my mom and yet, I was able to persuade her to let me go live with Dad in Cotati, California, if only for that summer.

# 1964-1966 COTATI, CA, CLEARFIELD, UT, & DURANGO, CO (1964 – 1965 10th Grade) (1965 - 1966 11th Grade)

About two weeks later, the entire family took me to the Greyhound bus station in Memphis. Mom handed me a brown paper bag containing three bologna (back then it was known as "blonie") sandwiches. J.C. gave me $3 and a pat on the back.

I had the clothes on my back plus two shirts, two pairs of underwear and one additional pair of jeans as well as the only pair of shoes that I owned on my feet. The trip from Memphis to San Francisco was three days by Greyhound bus. I was fourteen years old.

When I got on the bus, it was filled to its capacity. The only seat available was on the back seat. There was already one young man sitting against the window on that seat. He was a young black boy about my age. This kid didn't have any luggage or a brown paper bag.

I was accustomed to seeing black people and yet, I had never talked or spoken to any except for Snooks and his wife back on Mr. Well's farm. Our interaction was awkward at first.

It didn't take long though, before all color, race, or predetermined value of one over the other simply disappeared.

On that first day, I shared one of my sandwiches with him. I refer to the young man as "him" because I'm ashamed to say that I cannot remember his name. We had a great time sharing our stories, which were not that dissimilar, except the racial issues that impacted his life. For some reason, he didn't talk about that. I believe that we actually became friends.

One of our long stops was in Dallas, Texas. When we arrived at the bus station in Dallas, we had a two- three-hour layover prior to moving on to other points west. We were told by the bus driver that we could go anywhere we wanted, as long as we were back in time to board the bus prior to departure.

There were very few fast-food places at the time and there were none within walking distance of the Greyhound bus station. My new friend and I decided to walk down the block in search of a place to eat. We found a very simple mom and pop café or diner with only a screen door to enter. I walked in and expected my new friend to follow…he didn't.

I walked outside to find him sitting on the curb facing the street. I walked over and said, "I thought you were hungry, and I told you that I'd buy" …after all, I had $3 in my pockets. He didn't say anything and just pointed to a sign next to the entrance that simply said, "Whites only, colored around back."

This embarrassed me, pissed me off, and made me feel about 2' high. I went around back and purchased two hamburgers and one Coke at the colored only window and he and I sat on the curb, side by side, ate and shared the same bottle of Coke.

We got some strange looks from both white and black people walking by. We laughed and talked about the honky and the nigger boys sitting side by side just like there was nothing wrong with that at all.

I suppose that I'm fortunate that I didn't get strung up by a rope around my neck from the nearest lamp post that day; it simply didn't seem out of place to me.

Dear Reader, I trust that you can tell from this story that I've always hated racial prejudice of any kind. I thank God regularly for that chance meeting with that young black boy on the Greyhound bus bound for San Francisco in the summer of 1964.

We walked back to the bus, with me $1.20 poorer and re-boarded. I think we dropped my new friend off in Midland, Texas. I never saw him again nor can I remember his name, however I will never forget that experience. I think it was a "God thing" for me.

I remember crossing the Nevada-California state line and thinking, "This is not what I was expecting." There were no palm trees…only desert and tumbleweeds. Several hours later we rolled into the bus station in San Francisco.

The station was also different from what I was expecting…there were a dozen or so parking stalls for the buses and a covered platform leading to the terminal.

I got off the bus, picked up my ragged suitcase and headed toward the terminal. I spotted my stepmother first and she appeared to be horrified at my appearance…you must remember that I was a skinny, young kid who had not taken a bath in three days.

I was wearing the same clothes that I left Memphis in that weren't that great to begin with. Still, looking like I did, she hugged me and led me inside to find my dad. Dad loaded my ragged bag into a dark blue Ford Falcon.

We drove through the streets of San Francisco, across the Golden Gate Bridge and north to the little town of Cotati. Riding along the coast northward on Highway 101, I said to myself, "Now this is the California I was dreaming of."

We turned off the interstate onto West Sierra Avenue and almost immediately we turned left onto Juniper Drive. This was "Ernie's Trailer Park" which would be my home for the next ten months.

Other than the six years that I lived with my grandparents, this would be my longest tenure at any location until years later when I was stationed in Vietnam for twelve months.

Ernie was a real person. He was an Italian American who lived in San Francisco and came to Cotati on the weekends to maintain his trailer park. I would later work with Ernie for $1 per hour. He paid me cash, no taxes, etc.

The next day, my dad, stepmom, and I went back to San Francisco to a small Army base located at the Presidio. I think that the Presidio is now a park or recreation area.

In 1964, it was a very small base with a single paved air strip running parallel to the bay. The incoming or departing aircraft had to be very careful when approaching or departing to the west as it was very close to the Golden Gate Bridge. Our purpose for this trip was to get me a military dependent identification card. I still have that card.

After getting my I.D. card, we went to the PX (Post Exchange) to buy me some new clothes. I thought that I had died and gone to heaven!

While we were in San Francisco, we went to all the tourist sites: Fisherman's Wharf, Knob Hill, Chinatown, and looked through a powerful telescope at Alcatraz Island, on which there was a maximum security federal prison.

We visited a beach near the south end of the Golden Gate Bridge, and I walked in the sand and the surf. This was the first time that I had ever seen the ocean, except for riding over the Golden Gate Bridge the previous day. We also visited Fort Baker, located on the north end of the bridge just to the east.

There was a marina on Fort Baker and Dad, and I would spend many days fishing off of the docks there. I saw my first starfish, my first seal and caught my first saltwater fish (a toad fish) from these docks.

This was my first opportunity to see an ocean.
In this case, the Pacific Ocean, with my Dad.

Shortly after I arrived in Cotati, Ernie came up for the weekend. Ernie and I hit it off quickly and he asked me if I wanted a part-time job. I was so excited! I had worked all my life to this point and yet was never paid except for room and board, for which I was and still am very grateful.

So, I began working on Saturdays and Sundays with Ernie and after a couple of weekends, he started giving me a "to do list" for the following week.

He only asked that I not work more than twenty hours during the week. He trusted me to be honest with the time I turned in, he never complained and apparently was very happy with what I did. He always paid me in cash.

Ernie owned an Italian sandwich shop in San Francisco and on the weekends; he would bring a huge Italian sub-sandwich for lunch each day for both him and me. He also brought plenty of beer for us to wash it down with.

I worked for Ernie part-time for the entire ten months that I was in California. I never saw or talked to Ernie after I left California and yet, we had some great times working together. Ernie was a small man, and he knew the value of hard work.

My grandfather had taught me how to work hard at a very early age; I simply never knew any other way. It was a profitable habit for my US Marine Corps service and entire working career.

One day, Ernie and I were working on the landscaping on the side of the entrance to the park. We heard a loud crash and turned just in time to see the rear end of a car falling to the ground. West Sierra Avenue was a narrow paved road lined on each side with huge Eucalyptus trees. Eucalyptus trees are native to Australia and at some point, were imported to California.

These trees can grow to enormous size and are a very hard wood tree. Ernie and I both ran to the car and found a man slumped over the wheel, the steering wheel was broken, and his jawbone was protruding from his face, blood was everywhere.

He was mumbling something that we couldn't understand at first and then I spotted an indentation in the metal dashboard about the size of a softball.

We rolled the man over and a toddler was laying on the floor with his entire face smashed almost to the back of his head. Ernie ran to the nearest house to call for an ambulance and yet, there was no hope for the little boy.

The man survived. The child died with me trying to hold his head up to allow him to breathe. Seat belts were not required, and I doubt if they were even installed in most cars.

Apparently, the little boy was standing in the seat next to his dad and he tried to open the door, his dad reached to grab him, and the car left the road at no more than 30 MPH. Eucalyptus trees don't move.

Part of the engine was inside the car. I believe that experience helped make me the careful driver that I am, even to this day.

That summer passed much too quickly for me. It was nearing the time for me to go back to live with my mom and stepfather. I did not want to do that.

After much pleading with my dad and my mom, they finally agreed to let me stay for the coming school year. I hate to say this, and I don't mean any disrespect to my mom, however, she agreed only after my dad agreed to continue paying child support while I was living with him.

The school year that followed was the absolute best of my entire life. Once my mom agreed for me to spend the rest of the year with my dad, I enrolled in Rohnert Park High School.

This was a brand-new, modern school. It only went through the 10th grade and was built in typical California style. The campus was basically a square compound with a gate at the front entrance and at the back exit to the athletic facilities.

The lockers were located outside under an awning that encompassed two thirds of the outdoor wall space. All entrances to the classrooms were from the outside, no long interior halls, etc.

The gym, cafeteria and shop were located within the walled compound. There was an open outdoor meeting space with a concrete stage and tiered concrete seating that half circled the stage. Californians love their outdoor space, and it was perfect for me.

The school had four outdoor tennis courts, a full track, a football field, a baseball field, and a full-size Olympic swimming pool. I had to take tennis lessons as one of my PE classes. I hated tennis then and I still don't play. That's the only thing that I didn't like about Rohnert Park High School.

My father, Hynton Carliss Young, and me at a picnic table behind their mobile home in Ernie's Trailer Park, Cotati, California, 1964.

Rohnert Park Yearbook for 1964 – 1965.

Like I said, this was the first year for this school. Why this was so important to me was that everyone was a new student, just like I'd been my entire life. No one had the advantage of tenure and/or predetermined classifications in any sport

The first sport of the year was football. I absolutely loved playing football and especially at Rohnert Park. Although we only went through the tenth grade, we played a full ten game schedule with other schools in northern California that were full four-year schools. Our final record was 5/5 and we were proud of that record under the circumstances.

One of my favorite memories during a game was when we were playing Napa High School. It rarely rains very hard in this part of California and yet, on this night, it poured. I don't think they engineered the field for this amount of rain because it's so rare.

It started raining before kick-off and it never stopped. When we came out of the locker room after half-time, the officials asked if either team wanted to stop the game, neither did.

There was at least 1-2" of water on the field that wasn't going anywhere. We finished the game but one of the officials had to place the ball and hold his foot on it until the center got hands on it, otherwise the ball would

float away. I don't remember who won the game, and yet, it was some of the most fun I've ever enjoyed playing any sort of sport.

One of my closest friends was John Proctor. John dated (went steady with) Bernice Aquillon. They were the couple that everyone wanted to be. John had a brand-new Honda 90. This was the motorcycle that every boy in the school wanted, and it cost a whopping $400.

We weren't quite old enough to drive an automobile, so a motorcycle was a fantastic substitute, especially in northern California. Prior to the Honda 90, John had a 1958 Cushman motor scooter. It wasn't a Honda 90, but it was affordable, and I bought it for $75, against my dad's advice.

One day, it snowed in the mountains to the east of Cotati. This was an unusual event for this part of the state. The area surrounding Cotati and Rohnert Park was mostly sheep ranching in the early 1960's and most of the mountain (large hill) roads were narrow, paved asphalt.

Most ranches were fenced, and where the fence crossed the paved roads, they constructed what was known as a cattle gap. These were constructed with a bridge-type of structure made of railroad tracks. The tracks were placed four or five inches apart and perpendicular to the roadway. The livestock would not attempt to cross these structures thus no gates were needed, and traffic could move freely.

The day that it snowed, John and another friend named John Rea and I decided to ride up to the snow. John and John rode on his Honda 90, I was alone on my Cushman. I had been having some trouble with my brakes and didn't have the money to repair them, so I decided that I could easily stop, if required, by simply dragging my Beatle-style boots. Beatle boots were all the rage at the time. They were simply high-top dress

boots with a high heel and zipped on one side, very cool.

We were almost to the snow when my scooter started to overheat. We stopped for a while to allow it to cool down. By the time the engine cooled down it was starting to get dark and California law wouldn't allow anyone without a driver's license to drive a motor vehicle of any sort after dark, so we decided to head back down the mountain.

For the benefit of those dear readers who do not know what kick starting a motorcycle is, it's simply that you start the bike rolling down hill, place the bike in gear, release the clutch and theoretically, the engine will start.

No one had enlightened me with the knowledge that this procedure doesn't work when you have a centrifugal clutch. Basically, I was going downhill very fast on a narrow, winding paved road with no engine, no lights, and no brakes.

THE NEW HONDA 90
BRIDGES THE POWER GAP

My 1958 Cushman Road King.

The Beatle boots may have worked fine on flat ground at minimum speeds; however, they didn't work at all under these circumstances. We'll never know how fast the bike hit the cattle gap while sliding sideways, but it was enough to flip the bike and its rider. When I woke up, I was lying in a ditch with John Rea bending over me. I believe that he was praying; I know that he was crying.

He and the other John thought I was dead. I should have been. Helmets were not required, and I didn't own one. I had a nasty bruise on my head but no cuts. I was wearing a pair of white denim jeans, a football jersey and my most prized possession, my football letterman's jacket and of course, what was left of my Beatle boots.

I had no broken bones and no lasting effects from the accident. I did learn a valuable life lesson concerning proper maintenance of anything mechanical, and a healthy respect for motor bikes.

My jeans were completely torn off, my football jersey was ripped down the front and exposed my bleeding chest, but my football jacket only had a small two-inch square burn on one sleeve. The bike had done its last ride.

My dad was at a temporary duty station out of state...thank God! Only my stepmom was home when we got there. John and John had dropped me off at the front door before my stepmom came to it. I must have looked like a mess because she almost fainted when she saw me.

I never went to the doctor or the hospital, but the next two weeks, I felt like a zombie. Every part of my body ached. I've since owned three other motorcycles and I've always treated them with the utmost respect.

The only sport other than football that I participated in at Rohnert Park was track and field. I loved to run the one-hundred-yard dash, high jump, hurdles, and pole vaulting.

The first time I ever kissed a girl, or I should say, that a girl kissed me was in Cotati. This girl was not a girlfriend or anyone that I had given much thought to. Her name was Leah Ann Bickel.

Leah Ann was a redhead who loved to wear a lot of makeup and provocative clothes. She lived in a trailer park on the opposite side of West Sierra Avenue. Each morning, she, along with a half dozen others, walked to a common bus stop near the entrance to Ernie's trailer park.

One morning, we arrived near the bus stop at the same time. Out of the blue and without warning she walked up to me, pressed her massive breasts to my chest and planted one (a kiss) on me, I thought I really

needed to come up for air.

I don't know why she did that and she never did it again but that was my introduction to "French kissing." Hell, it was my first kiss ever. I was in a daze for the rest of the day, week, maybe month. Obviously, it left a lasting impression on me.

Another girl who lived in the same trailer park as Leah Ann was a girl by the name of Lisa Rea. She was John Rea's sister, and they were both adopted. John and I played football and ran track together. Lisa and I learned the fine art of making out together. Lisa and I never really dated, per say, but we did find a lot of opportunities to be alone.

The first girl I can say that I dated (went "steady" with) was Anna Jaeck. Anna and her mom lived alone in an apartment complex in Rohnert Park. Her mom and dad were divorced and yet, apparently, he took care of them very well. Going to her house was the first time (I'm not going where you thought I was) I'd ever seen the inside of an apartment complex. For me, they were living very well indeed.

Anna's father worked on an oil rig in the Gulf of Mexico. Her mom was a nurse in a hospital in Santa Rosa, just a few miles north of Cotati. We had a typical early high school romance, participated in high school dances, etc. Her mom usually gave us rides.

I would walk home from school most of the time; Anna's apartment was about halfway. I would stop for a couple of hours and we would do homework together. (There you go thinking again...).

My very best academic school year was my sophomore year, 1964-65. Each semester they would publish a principal's list of the top ten academic students in the school and I made the list the entire year. I once made it all the way to number 2. See, those homework sessions with Anna really helped.

That's my story and I'm sticking to it!

My girlfriend, Anna Jaeck, and me
in Rohnert Park High School.

My problems at the plethora of other schools I attended was the fact that when you move so often, you don't have the time or the desire to meet and make new friends because you know it's only a matter of time before you'll be leaving. It's inevitable that the new school will academically be either ahead of or behind the school you previously attended.

It's discouraging to either have to wait for the new class to catch up to you or having to work your butt off trying to catch up. Like I said earlier, Rohnert Park was all new, no one had to catch up and all of us, for the most part, were strangers. I also had those tutoring sessions in Rohnert Park with Anna.

Another situation when moving so much was, at least from the male side of the equation, that around this time in a young man's life, he has raging hormones, and it seems like every male in school wants to establish his turf.

The Alpha male in ALL high schools does this best, and what better way to do that than to seek out the new guy and beat his butt just to show the newbie who's boss. (If you have ever watched "Animal Kingdom" on the National Geographic channel, you will understand what I mean.)

It eventually got to the point where soon after getting enrolled in a new school, I would be the aggressor and seek out and locate the Alpha male and do my best to kick his butt and get that out of the way. It should be noted that I never lost any of those battles except in the seventh grade. That's a story for another time.

One other short story before we move away from California: This incident occurred while Billie Steve was home on leave from the Navy. Billie Steve was stationed in Hawaii, poor soul…….but I digress!

Dad owned a 1954 Chevrolet convertible. Billie Steve and I talked Dad into letting us borrow the car to drive to Santa Rosa, only eight miles or so to the north of Cotati. Dad agreed; however, he gave us strict instructions not to take his prized car on the interstate, we both agreed. This interstate highway was California Highway 101 or the Redwood Highway.

When we pulled out of Ernie's Trailer Park, we should have turned left but no, we turned right and then directly onto the ramp to the interstate northbound for Santa Rosa. Billie Steve may remember the event differently but I'm sure I'm right: it was Billie Steve's idea.

We had the top down and were really enjoying our little trip to Santa Rosa, when suddenly, the hood blew up and over the top of the car. Obviously, when we stopped for gas and to check the oil, someone forgot to make sure the latch was secure. Billie Steve stopped the car, and we retrieved the hood.

Billie Steve's first thought was that we could go by the hardware store and purchase a rubber mallet and a can of spray paint. We could fix this, and no one would be the wiser---duh, you'd think that Billie

Steve was from Mississippi.

We finally put what was left of the hood in the back seat and slowly went back home. Amazingly enough, Dad wasn't angry. Billie Steve and I both breathed a sigh of relief. I think Dad greatly loved Billie Steve; Dad didn't know me that well.

The moral of this story is that you can go to the Dairy Queen (DQ) with Billie Steve but not the interstate.

Shortly after I arrived in California to live with my dad and stepmother, my sister Sharon came to live with us. She also brought her little two-year-old daughter, Debbie Langston. This was the first time that I'd met Debbie. I'm not sure why but for some reason I called her Dee-Dee, that has stuck to this day.

For some reason nicknames are a thing in the South. When they first got to our house, Dee-Dee wouldn't have a thing to do with me. I tried everything I could think of to make her like me, but nothing worked. One day, I was going to the mailbox located near the entrance to the trailer park and Sharon asked me to take Dee-Dee with me.

She didn't want to go with me, but her mother insisted. I took her, kicking and screaming, placed her on my shoulders and walked to the mailbox. She loved it. After that, I couldn't get rid of her. Dee-Dee now lives in Augusta, Georgia near her two children and grandchildren.

The year was 1965, my dad was a career soldier, the war in Vietnam was heating up. My dad received his orders for his first of three one-year tours of duty in Vietnam.

My stepmom didn't want to be responsible for a teenage boy with raging hormones and a propensity to do stupid stuff like riding a bike down a mountain with no brakes. So, my good life was about to end abruptly.

For the record, I don't blame my stepmom in any way. I'm certain that my mother wouldn't have allowed me to stay even if my stepmom wanted me to do so. However, it was one of the most difficult events in my life to that point when I had to board that Greyhound bus in downtown Cotati, California, and ride it all the way to Salt Lake City, Utah.

Just for the record, one of my football coaches (Coach Tuthill) and my shop teacher (Mr. Benton) offered to let me spend the remainder of that school year living with them, but my mother wouldn't allow it.

While I was living in California, my stepfather had "surrendered" to the ministry. He was ordained and sent to serve a small church in Clearfield, Utah.

My fellow Rohnert Park teammates.

(L-R) Mr. Benton, Shop Teacher, and Coach Tuthill.

Obviously, it didn't take very long to educate and qualify a Southern Missionary Baptist preacher in those days. Clearfield is located about midway between Salt Lake City and Ogden, Utah.

One of the people seeing me off at the bus station was Anna Jaeck. Anna gave me a wrapped present just before I boarded the bus and asked me to not open it until the bus had pulled out of the station.

I waved goodbye to my stepmother, Sharon, and Anna. I knew better, however, we all pretended that it was just a matter of time and I'd be returning. It was all that I could do to not cry.

Once the bus was heading south in the direction of San Francisco, I opened the present and was blown away---it was a Playboy magazine! I was embarrassed but I did not throw it away.

Remember those raging hormones? Of course, the only reason that I wanted the magazine was for the men's clothes that were in the ads. Now, if you believe that, I still have that very attractive Alpine property in Miami that I'll give you a great deal on.

A few years later, in early 1969, I was passing through Rohnert Park on my way to Santa Rosa. I was stationed in Southern California and a friend and I were going to" pick up his car from his parent's home in Santa Rosa. I called Anna to see if I could drop by for a few minutes. She said, "Sure." I went over and spent a couple of hours at her apartment.

It's sort of strange but I learned that one should never go back and try to recreate something that never was in the first place. She was in her second year of college at Sonoma State University and I was in the Marine Corps. We were now galaxies apart in our thinking and politics. It was an awkward evening and after saying our goodbyes once again, I never saw or talked to her again.

Back to my departure from Cotati: The next day, we were rolling across the Great Salt Lake and into Salt Lake City, Utah. My mom, stepdad, sister, Deb, and my little brother, Jay, were at the bus station to greet me and take me the eight miles or so north to my new home in Clearfield.

Boyd had joined the Army during my absence. Our house in Clearfield was, by far, the nicest house that I'd ever lived in. It was modern and situated in a subdivision.

Our house was directly next door to a Mormon bishop and his family's home. Believe it or not, the bishop had three daughters with whom he did his best to hook me up. I was so depressed that I simply wasn't interested. I'd simply take my old, worn-out Playboy magazine and look at the ads.

I did go over one night when the sisters were babysitting for some friends while the girls' parents went to some church event. I was informed where the liquor cabinet was located as well as the location of the bedrooms. I didn't take advantage of either. It was obvious that I was seriously depressed.

Some friends at J.C.'s church owned a horse ranch and invited me to visit on Sunday afternoons between services. I had ridden horses all of my life and this was a great way to clear my mind and just get away.

I was able to participate in a junior rodeo at calf roping and barrel riding. I don't remember how I did in either event, but I don't think I won any prizes. In Utah, in those days, the kids were raised on horseback.

As soon as I got settled after the bus trip from San Francisco, I went to enroll in the local high school. The administrator took my records and compared where we were in California with where they were and concluded that I was far ahead of them and it would serve no purpose for me to go to school for just a few weeks. So, she passed me onto the eleventh grade without attending any classes.

I suppose I was never actually a student in Utah because I never attended any classes. However, I was enrolled, so in my book, it counts as one of my twenty- two schools.

I'm sure by now that you are aware that this DACBFM was in the habit of doing stupid things. Utah was no exception to this rule. Where we lived, if you took away all of the buildings and landscaping, you would find yourself basically in a desert. The soil was very coarse sand and wouldn't support much in the way of grass or plants without a lot of irrigation.

One day, shortly after I arrived in Clearfield, I was watering plants in the backyard when I discovered that if you turned the water faucet wide open, you could basically push the hose as far down into the ground as you wished. I pushed and pushed and finally the walls of my little experiment collapsed. The hose was irretrievable.

I was sure that if my stepfather were to find out what a stupid thing I'd done, he would have worn out his belt on my back side. I did the only thing I knew to do, I started digging and digging and digging.

Eventually, I was hanging only by my feet on the side of the huge hole. I finally got the hose free. I had barely gotten my body out of the hole when the sides collapsed. Had I been just a few seconds longer, I would have looked like the local Ute Indians had planted me upside down in the sand. Once again, God had some reason for this DACBFM to live.

This part of the state of Utah was noted for its vegetable farming so I got a part-time job picking strawberries with the intent to purchase a Honda 90 by the end of the summer. Do you have a clue how many strawberries one would have to pick in order to earn $400 dollars? I think by working all summer or at least the part of it that we were in Utah, I may have earned a total of $40-60.

Once again, I was heartbroken and had very sore knees from crawling down those rows of strawberries. The only people in those fields were many Mexican migrant farm workers and me, a stupid white boy from Mississippi. Now, I could add picking strawberries to my growing resume of farm work. I picked cotton and sorted sweet potatoes in Mississippi, and loaded baled hay in Durango, Colorado.

Let's not forget the landscaping in California and working as a dishwasher and busboy in Colorado and Arkansas. I also worked at a steakhouse in Augusta, Georgia as a short-order cook. I was really building my resume, wasn't I?

My stepfather had purchased a 1964 Chevrolet Impala. I haven't a clue how he could afford it but he bought it. It was red and black on the outside with mag wheels. It had black and red tuck and roll interior with four on the floor (I'm not talking about a double date here) and a big four-barrel Holly carburetor. It was very "boss" (that means "cool").

Obviously, Southern Missionary Baptist preachers in Utah were paid well. I had turned sixteen and it was time for me to get my driver's license. My mom took me into Salt Lake City to take my test.

I passed the written test with ease, however, when the instructor and I went for the actual driving part of the test, he had me drive out of town and we stopped on a deserted country road. He asked me to see if I could "lay down rubber."

I could, and I did. He immediately flunked me and told me to never break the law simply because someone in authority told me to do so. That pissed me off. I came back in a week or so and re-took that part of the exam and passed. This time when he asked me to gun it, I just looked at him and said, "Seriously?!"

Before school was scheduled to start, we moved to Durango, Colorado. I never knew why, however, we moved without the Impala.

My stepfather had bought some "Junker" piece of crap car and that's what we all rode in, along with all our earthly belongings, into Colorado.

We moved into the same apartments that we had lived in back when I was in the third grade. This was the old motel complex where all the original motel units had been converted into apartments.

I enrolled in Durango High School and became a Blue Demon, our mascot. Football was difficult that year. It was a large school and the competition was fierce. I got some playing time, however, I was a newbie and ranked way down on the pecking order. It was not one of my best years.

After football season, I took part in the wrestling team. Mainly because they had a difficult time recruiting boys who wanted to wear those tights and swap sweat with other guys. I wasn't crazy about that part, but I needed something to blow off steam. I did well in the competition, however it simply wasn't enough to hold my interest.

My grades suffered and I lost all interest in school. I ran away from home once. I started walking and hitchhiking west over the mountains in the direction of California. I haven't a clue what I would have done had I made it.

I didn't have a bag of clothes or even a heavy jacket. About halfway from Durango and Cortez, Colorado, it started to snow, the wind blew, and the temperature dropped so fast that I thought I'd freeze to death.

A man heading back in the direction of Durango stopped and gave me a ride back home. My mom and stepfather never knew of that little adventure.

One of the guys that I'd met and went to school with lived in a small trailer located a few hundred yards behind our apartment. He was one of the few people I knew who was poorer than we were. He lived in this trailer with his mother. I went in the trailer only once; it was so cluttered that you couldn't even sit down. It would be a stretch to say that we were friends, however he was someone to hang out with, so we'll call him a friend.

His name was Bill Sapp. Bill fancied himself a cowboy; he wore old blue jeans, cowboy boots, cowboy shirts, a belt with a huge buckle and a cowboy hat that had seen its best days many years earlier.

He and I climbed rock faces, without the proper equipment, went on long hikes in the mountains and he once helped me drag a young elk off the mountain. I was hunting mule deer by myself with a 30/30 Winchester that I had borrowed from my stepfather, and the young elk simply got in the wrong place at the right time.

The elk was way too large for me to get off the mountain by myself, so Bill helped. Bill also knew how to process the elk and at that time, I had never cleaned anything larger than a raccoon.

There are two stories worth telling concerning Bill Sapp: One day Bill simply disappeared. No one knew where he had gone or if he ever intended to return. His mom showed no concern at all. I suppose that she knew that he could take care of himself, or maybe it was because with him gone, she didn't have to worry about feeding and housing him.

One day, a detective from the Durango police department gave me a visit at our home. They had found a body in the mountains not far from the main highway and they couldn't identify it.

Somehow, they had put two and two together and were trying to connect Bill's disappearance and his and my relationship to the situation. They asked me to come down to the morgue to see if I could identify the body of the young man.

This was the first time that I'd ever seen a dead body other than at a funeral. The coroner asked me to stand on a ladder directly above the body and see if I could identify it. The body had been in the woods for over a week before it was discovered, it also had a bullet wound in the right temple. I could not confirm that it was or was not Bill Sapp.

The detective must have questioned me for two or three hours. I was feeling extremely uncomfortable. It was obvious to me that they thought this was Bill and that I'd had something to do with his death. After a long afternoon and strict orders not to leave the Durango area, they sent me home.

I think my mom may have also suspected that I'd had something to do with Bill's disappearance because she questioned me all the way home. She kept saying, "Pee-Wee, if you had anything to do with this, please tell me." I told her that I did not and all she did was cry.

A few weeks later, while I was working in the front yard, probably picking up rocks because we didn't have any grass, I heard someone approaching me. I looked around and, lo and behold, it was Bill Sapp! He said something like, "Man, you look like you've just seen a ghost." I told him that I had and that he was it.

The second Bill Sapp story: My stepfather was operating a gas station in Durango. It was a typical gas station of the day. It had a single bay garage for working on vehicles and two gas pumps in front.

One pump was for regular gas and the other was "high test," or as it was referred to then as "ethyl" gasoline. It wasn't unusual for me to come to the station after school and run it while J.C. went home for supper. He would return later; I would go home and he would mind the station until closing time.

One day, I was minding the station and business was slow. I was sitting behind a small desk in the station with my feet propped on the desk when in walked Bill and another boy who I did not know. Bill pulled a 22-caliber pistol out of his pocket and shouted, "Give us everything that's in the register!"

Without thinking, I reached up and snatched the pistol out of his hand and shouted back, "Hell no!" The other boy ran out of station without even saying goodbye, which I thought was rather rude.

Bill looked at me with fear in his eyes. I realized at that moment that they weren't kidding. It was a real weapon and they indeed wanted to rob me. I'm not sure what they were going to do because it was obvious that I knew Bill.

Later, the thought occurred to me that the only logical outcome to that situation was if I was eliminated. Now that certainly would have upset me. At any rate, I told Bill to get out of my sight and I kept the pistol. I don't remember what eventually happened to the pistol, and yet, it is no longer in my possession.

On a more positive note, the only girl that I dated in Durango was Ann Brown. Ann was a very petite girl with brown eyes and short brown hair, the haircut was called a "pixie" at the time. She and her family lived just on the outskirts of Durango in an unpainted frame house.

Her mother was a better than average cook and her father was a more than average alcoholic. Ann taught me three things: how to snow ski, ice skate and drink like you really liked it.

I was at her home for one holiday and her mother cooked an incredible meal and her father and I drank an incredible amount of whiskey. I also remember being incredibly sick the next day. My drinking experiences had started much earlier in life and yet, this was the first time in my memory that I had set out to get stone-faced drunk.

I later had a part time job at a locally owned steakhouse. This was my first of many jobs in restaurants. Restaurant work was easy to get and once you worked at one you knew why...it was difficult work. I worked as a dishwasher two nights a week for 75 cents an hour.

On rare occasions the waitresses would throw me a small portion of their tips. Back then, they were known as waitresses, not servers. One of the other guys who worked a different shift than me, had, of all things, a Honda 90.

I had gotten into fly fishing and this friend would let me borrow his Honda 90 while he was working so that I could go to a favorite fishing stream. I would spend hours fishing for rainbow trout. I would ride the Honda as far as the trail would allow and then I would walk down to the stream. It was total solitude and pure enjoyment for a troubled young man.

I only got into one fight while in Durango. I rode the bus to school and one morning the only seat that was vacant was next to a young Mexican girl. I sat down not thinking anything of it, but I later learned that it was taboo for a white boy to sit next to a Mexican girl.

One of the Mexican boys started picking a fight, the bus driver said, with authority, for us to wait until we were off the bus. We waited and once off the bus we agreed to meet behind the gym.

For some stupid reason, I was carrying that pistol that I had taken away from Bill Sapp. Luckily, I gave it to a friend prior to going behind the gym. As I turned the corner of the gym and was removing my coat, the Mexican boy came at me with both fists.

It took me a few seconds to get my bearings and finish removing my coat. Once I got my coat off and was able to defend myself, I was already bleeding heavily from my mouth and nose. I was finally able to get into the fight, we were both bleeding and blood covered the snow in a ten-foot circle.

A crowd had gathered but suddenly, two huge hands reached down and pulled both of us backward. They were the hands of the principal of the school. I believe both of us were glad to have someone end the fight. It's likely that one of us would have died had it been allowed to continue.

We were both ordered to go to the principal's office, which we did. We were given a firm warning and he dismissed the Mexican boy. He told me to stay (after all, I was the newbie). Once we were alone, he asked me if I had an issue with Mexicans.

I told him that I didn't. I told him about my non-prejudiced stance concerning any race or religion. He gave me a long dissertation on proper conduct, etc. and let me go with only a warning.

When I left the principal's office and neared the end of the hall the Mexican boy was standing there waiting for me. I think my first thought must have been "Oh crap, here we go again."

To my surprise, he stuck out his hand. He took my hand and apologized for being such an ass. We laughed about parts of the fight and were on good terms from then on. That macho testosterone is some strange crap. You can substitute the word "shit" for crap if you like. That's what I wanted to say but was considerate of the young people who may, by some miracle, read this.

J.C. bought a new 1964 Plymouth Fury. It wasn't fancy and yet, it did have an automatic transmission and four doors. It was simply a family car. One day, I was going on a trip to the local auto parts store for J.C. and I took the Plymouth.

I pulled out of the gas station and for some reason, I didn't see a huge Budweiser beer truck…it rammed into the driver's side. The accident didn't prevent the automobile from being driven but it did add to my depression.

By this time, I was cutting school a lot and I had no interest in school or relationships. I desperately wanted to be back in California, but that simply wasn't going to happen. One of my earliest life lessons was this: most of the time when we long for something that we've lost, it's only the concept that we want, not the actual person, place, or thing. Rarely are they as we remember them. Had I been able to go back to California, it still wouldn't have been the same. Life moves on.

My stepmother had moved to Fort Rucker, Alabama, so returning to Cotati wasn't even possible. My dad had shipped out to Vietnam. My shop teacher and my assistant football coach in California wanted me to move in with them but my mother wouldn't have it .

In desperation, I convinced my mother to sign for me to go into the military service. I don't know why we chose to go to the Navy recruiter, but I will always be grateful that we did. I was desperate to get away from where I was. I guess I thought I would be stationed in California.

When we sat down with the Navy Recruiter and he was reviewing my school records, he closed his file, looked me squarely in the face and said, "Kid, I will not sign you up now. However, if you finish high school, I'll do my best to get you an appointment to the Naval Academy."

I should have been very proud of what he was suggesting, however, once again, I was devastated. I struggled to catch up at school with little success. My heart simply wasn't in it. I'd just about come to the end of my wits. I must admit that I was having serious suicidal thoughts.

J.C. started preaching at a small church about fifty miles west in Cortez, Colorado. For a while, we drove from Durango to Cortez each Sunday and Wednesday. We would remain in Cortez on Sunday afternoons in order to be able to attend church Sunday evening.

We would drive the one-hundred-mile round trip on Wednesdays to attend a one-hour prayer meeting. After a short time, we moved to Cortez. We lived in a mobile home that was a huge upgrade from the motel apartment in Durango. I transferred to Cortez High School.

One of my most prized possessions was my letterman's jacket from Rohnert Park High in California. I was walking down the hall at my new school and this big, ugly guy wearing a Cortez High School letterman's jacket approached me. He said, "Kid, you can't wear that crap in this school."

I told him that it was from another state, another time and it could mean no disrespect to his school or team. He said that it made no difference, if I wore it again, the entire football team was going to kick my butt. I didn't have an issue with fighting just one person.

The letters from my Rohnert Park High School football letterman's jacket.

However, the entire football team was a little too much of a challenge. I humbled myself and never wore the jacket to school again. That pit of depression just kept getting deeper and deeper. As that pit grew deeper, my consumption of alcohol increased.

When we lived in Durango and I was working, I bought a twenty-two semi-automatic rifle. I still own this weapon today and it's displayed in my gun case right beside the wet bar. That's where all gun cases should be located, right?

While living in Cortez, I would spend some of my spare time walking on the prairie and shooting prairie dogs. The ranchers would gladly allow you to come on their property to shoot them.

The prairie dogs would dig large holes or burrows and it was common for horses or cattle to step in these holes and break a leg. Once that happened, the rancher had to destroy the animal.

My stepfather once again bought a car that there was no way he could afford. It was a 1966 Buick Skylark. This car was not a hot rod like the Impala he had in Utah. It was a baby blue and white on the outside with white tuck and roll interior.

This was a beautiful car and he let me use it a few times for dates. I dated a couple of girls in Cortez but the life of me, I can't remember their names. It was interesting that almost all of the girls I dated, after the third date, wanted to go home with me and meet my parents. Well, that wasn't going to happen, not because I was ashamed of my parents, but I was embarrassed of where we lived.

Once I became aware of the trend, it was three dates and you are out of here. I often wonder how many of them simply thought that I was a snob. Some of these girls were obviously hurt however I simply didn't possess the social skills to explain why, nor would my pride allow it. I learned to live with it. This could be the reason that I'm perceived as insensitive to this day. That's my excuse and I'm sticking to it!

It didn't take long before we were pulling up stakes and moving back east. J.C. bought an old Datsun pickup truck and an 8' x 30' trailer (A mobile home known as a 1960 "Rollohome"). As difficult as it is to visualize, we hooked this trailer to the back of the Datsun truck and pulled it all the way from Cortez, Colorado to Haynes, Arkansas. J.C. had taken a job as the new pastor of the Haynes Baptist Church.

This trip was a total distance of a little over twelve hundred miles. We took the Buick with us. We must have looked like the Oklahoma land rush in reverse or the Beverly Hillbillies.

An interesting point: the Rollohome trailer was 240 square feet total and there were five of us who lived in it for one year. When I retired from Thomas and Hutton, my office was 360 square feet. Everything in life needs to be viewed from its own perspective. Most of our lives we want a whole lot more than we need.

It really upsets me when I hear couples who own a three thousand square foot house with three bedrooms and two and a half baths and two children telling me, "We have to find a larger house. This one is simply too small for our family." Seriously??

Haynes Baptist Church, Haynes, Arkansas, where we lived next door in the 8' x 30' Rollohome mobile home / trailer that we pulled from Cortez, Colorado.

**See what comfort really is**

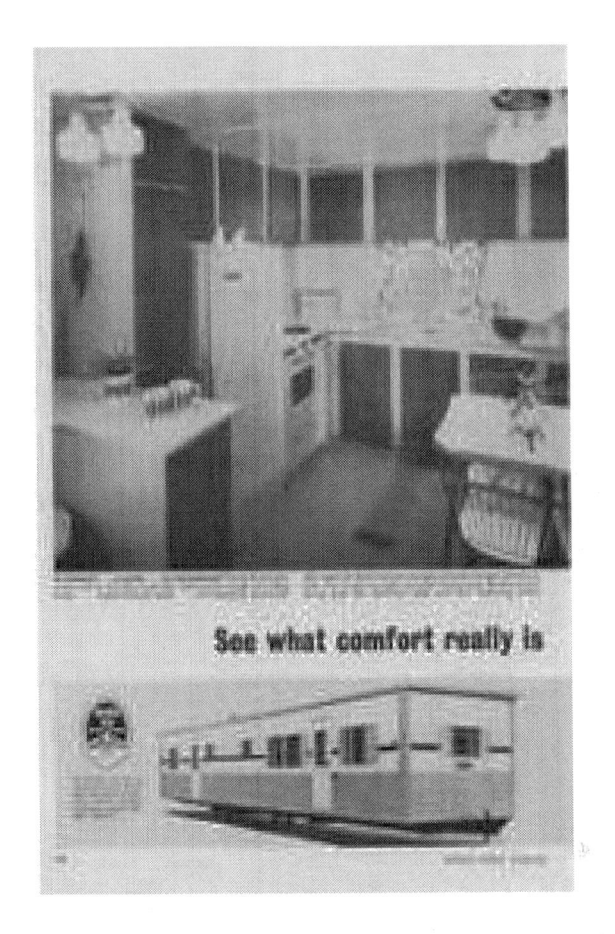

　　While living in Haynes, Arkansas and after purchasing my first automobile, a 1960 Rambler American, for some unknown reason, J.C. said, "If you take Jay with you, I will let you use the Buick Skylark." I will probably never know why he did that. J.C. loved that Skylark, and he rarely allowed me to use it, especially after I had purchased the Rambler.

I drove Jay to Forest City in the Skylark to see a movie. I was able to find a parking spot directly in front of the movie theater. When the movie was over, we walked outside to drive home, and the car was not where I had parked it.

All that was there were some blue paint chips and broken glass. The man at the ticket counter gave me a phone number and allowed me to use the theater phone (remember, no cell phones yet. Those weren't to come along for another forty or so years.)

The phone number was to the local police station; the sheriff came to pick us up in a patrol car and took us to the station. On the way to the station, he took us by a holding yard where we looked at a 1966 Buick Skylark that reminded me of a horseshoe.

About a block away from the theater and at the top of a steep hill was the local Post Office. Apparently, a truck parked on the top of hill, in front of the Post Office, had come down the hill unmanned and somehow missed all of the other cars and plowed into the side of the Buick.

I've always suspected that J.C. may have had something to do with this, however, I'm not sure how he would have pulled that off. He had no idea where I would park the Buick and he would have had to avoid all the other traffic in order to hit just the Buick.

The sheriff called J.C. and explained, in detail, what had happened. While J. C. was driving my Rambler to pick us up, the sheriff asked if he could do anything for me. I assume that he could see the fear on my face.

I told him that he could put me inside a jail cell and not let J.C. have the key. Surprisingly, J.C. wasn't upset at all. The three of us got in my Rambler and went home. I never heard another word concerning that car.

# 1966-1967 DURANGO, CO, CORTEZ, CO, & HAYNES, AR (1966-1967 12th Grade)

Boyd had quit school after his second attempt at the eighth grade. Boyd was not stupid by any stretch of the imagination. He was very sharp and creative. Boyd simply didn't adjust well to all of the moving and changing of schools.

It was very difficult to change homes, schools, friends, etc. as often as we did. Every school that we attended was at a different place in their classwork than the one we had just left.

The teachers of the 50's and 60's apparently had very little tolerance for students who weren't at the same level as the rest of their class, at least "that's my story and I'm sticking to it." There were exceptions, of course. Unfortunately, they were few and far between.

It wasn't until I was forced to move from my dad and stepmother's home in Cotati, California to Clearfield, Utah that I learned that Boyd had enlisted in the U.S. Army at the age of 17. My mom had to sign the authorization papers for him to join at that young age.

The Vietnam War was going strong by this time and Boyd was sent to serve in that arena. Boyd and my father were stationed at the same base at the same time in Vietnam. While fathers and sons serving in Vietnam at the same time wasn't that unusual, serving on the same base was extremely unusual.

When Boyd returned from Vietnam we were living in the small Rollohome parked next to the church in Haynes, Arkansas. When I say "we," I mean my mom, stepfather, sister Deb, little brother Jay and me.

I had worked the previous summer as a busboy at the Holiday Inn in Forest City, Arkansas. So, I had earned enough ($400) to buy my first automobile, a 1960 Rambler American. It was only a four-cylinder car that burned more oil than gas, but it was mine, and I was very proud of it.

One of its nicest features was that both front seats would recline all the way back. In this position, it was one large flatbed from the dash to the back of the car. This car was a teenage boy's dream come true. The car had two doors, all white on the outside and the inside upholstery was red and black checkerboard vinyl. The radio was AM only with a small dial in the middle of a large dial.

The small dial was for turning the radio off and on and controlling the volume; the larger, outside dial was for channel selection. I used to keep a case of oil in the trunk, when I stopped to fill the tank with gas, I'd always add a quart of oil.

Don't knock it, the car was mine and it was paid for. I honestly can't remember filling the car up with gas. A dollar would buy me at least five gallons of gas and I usually only put $2 worth of the cheap stuff in the tank.

Boyd obviously had a lot of energy and other issues to work out after serving in Vietnam. He asked me if he could borrow my car and, of course, I agreed. I didn't know where Boyd was going or what he planned to do. He didn't know anyone in Haynes because he'd never had the pleasure of living in this Arkansas paradise. I think he simply went out to drink and get Vietnam off his mind.

We didn't have a phone in the Rollohome trailer. Sometime during the middle of the early morning there was a knock on the front door. It was the sheriff. Our first thought was that Boyd was dead. Well, he wasn't, but my poor car was. He had had a few too many drinks, had lost control of the car and drove it into a cornfield somewhere between Marianna and Haynes, Arkansas.

Boyd was comfortably sleeping it off in the jail in Marianna. My prized car had been towed to the "holding pen" as they referred to at the sheriff's office. They did not charge Boyd with anything, and I believe that was because of his recent service in Vietnam, also, there were no other vehicles or drivers involved.

I never saw my car again. It needs to be noted that Boyd was still only 18 years old. I have no idea where Boyd bought his liquor, however, given my own personal experience, it wasn't that difficult for underage kids to purchase it in Haynes, Arkansas, especially if you had military identification.

Technically, my senior year of high school was spent attending Marianna High School, Marianna, Arkansas. Marianna was located about ten miles south of where we lived in Haynes. In addition to pastoring the Haynes Baptist Church, J.C. was also driving a semi-truck across the country from time to time.

We were living in the trailer next to the church. During Christmas break 1966, J.C. asked me if I would like to ride with him from Memphis to San Diego. I had just turned eighteen and was excited about the opportunity to at least see California again.

My mom dropped us off at the truck yard located in West Memphis, Arkansas and we fueled the Diamond Tee, ten speed road ranger, hooked to a trailer full of frozen chickens and started west.

I don't believe that we had even gotten out of Arkansas before we stopped and purchased a couple of six packs of Falstaff beer. These were the first two six packs of many that we would purchase before this little adventure was to be over.

The trip was issue-free, until we got on top of the mountains east of San Diego. J.C. was driving a bit too fast for the grade of the road, and his condition was impaired due to the quantity of Falstaff beers he had consumed. Please note, he never offered, nor did I drink a single beer on this trip.

I don't know how fast we were going when J.C. screamed, "We have no brakes!" The truth is that he had burned the brakes trying to slow down. We were building up speed fast, the smell of burning brake shoes was about to make me pass out. I was preparing to jump out of the semi at the first opportunity when J.C. started rubbing the right-side tires on the truck and the trailer against a curb.

It took miles before he was able to bring it to a safe stop. The cab of that truck probably still smells like an outhouse. He had to walk to a location to place a call for a tow truck to take us the rest of the way into San Diego.

He had to have all of the tires on the right side replaced as well as a full set of brakes and brake shoes. I can only imagine how much that cost. Maybe this explains why this was his last truck trip as far as I'm aware.

The fun was not over. We stayed in San Diego for a few days, sleeping in the truck, and finally we hooked to another trailer. This trailer was filled with heads of lettuce. We headed back east. Once we were safely over the mountains, we entered a flat, barren part of California and J.C. needed some rest so he turned the truck driving over to me.

I was eighteen, did not have a CDL license and had never had any training on a truck of this size. It didn't take too long before I was feeling comfortable behind the wheel. This was the first vehicle that I'd ever driven that was equipped with cruise control. Once you shifted through all of the ten gears and activated the cruise control, it was simple.

After a three to four hour nap, J.C. woke up and took over the controls. We were near the Mexico border by now and J.C. knew a place just south of the border that served breakfast.

The border was a simple place to cross back then. There was only a sign stating that you were leaving the USA and entering Mexico—no guards, no gates, nothing. After only a couple of miles, we pulled into the dirt parking lot of a roadside diner.

We went inside and there were only a few people eating. We sat down at the bar near an old, weathered Mexican cowboy-looking man. His skin was tanned, hard and wrinkled.

He was having what appeared to be a couple of fried eggs, some sort of Mexican hash, salt-cured ham, and jalapenos on the side. J.C. told the waitress that we would take two of the same.

It was awesome, until I bit into one of those peppers. I had never tasted anything that spicy in my life. I must have drunk a gallon of water. The old cowboy was eating them like they were breath mints! We finished our breakfast, minus the jalapenos, and we were back on the highway.

The next morning, after my morning "constitutional," I thought I would have to call the fire department! We made it home safely before Christmas.

I'm not sure why, but my sister Deb went to grade school in Hughes, Arkansas. Hughes was located twenty or so miles east of Marianna. When I still had my 1960 Rambler American, I would take her to school and then return to Marianna before my classes began. On one of these trips, it was raining, and it had been raining for days. The rice fields, which are common in this part of Arkansas, were flooded.

Due to the rain, we were traveling at, maybe, thirty miles per hour. I spotted something floating in one of the fields so I slowed down to see if I could identify it. It was the body of a black woman. Once I determined that she was dead, I drove into Hughes, Arkansas to the local police department to report what we had seen.

This was long before the invention of cell phones, so I really didn't have any other options. The kind police officer provided transportation for my sister to get to school. I'm not sure what her fellow students thought of her showing up for school in a police cruiser, but let's call it an "adventure."

I thought they would let me go back to school (and we know how much I loved school), but no. I had to go with the police officers to the location where we had seen the body. The policeman dragged the body of the woman up onto high ground and in the process found the body of a black man.

The police officer and I were both drenched to the bone. He called for a coroner to come pick up the bodies and transport them to the morgue in West Memphis. I had to go back to the police station in Hughes and spend half the day answering questions.

I suppose they were just doing their normal police thing. By the time they released me to go to school, classes were almost over. I went in to explain the day to the principal and I'm not sure that he ever bought my story. I actually don't think that he could have cared less. After all, I was the newbie who really didn't give a crap.

Eventually, we (my parents and I) were told that apparently, during a heated argument, the man had killed his wife using a butcher knife and then he drank some cotton poison to kill himself.

By this time in my life, I had started drinking much heavier than a young teenage boy should. It is my opinion that no teenage boy should be drinking at all. I suppose my excuse was that if it was good enough for my stepfather, it should be okay for me.

Before the San Diego trip, my mom would often accompany J.C. on his road trips. Debra, Jay, and I were left to fend for ourselves. While mom and J.C. were on one of these trips, some friends of mine were having a party at this girl's house.

I will have to withhold the names here to protect the guilty. This girl was extremely talented on the piano and she had a beautiful voice. Her parents were out of town, and we partied at her house.

One friend, Hayes Traylor, and I played football together and this night we drank way too much. We ran out of alcohol and decided to go to my house (the tiny trailer) to see if we could find some of J.C.'s "stash." We didn't find anything, so we mixed rubbing alcohol and ketchup with water. It's only by the grace of God that we both survived that night. At some point in the night, I took Hayes home.

Hayes lived in Marianna, and I lived in Haynes, a good ten miles apart. I was able to get Hayes home without incident. By the time I was halfway home, I was a sick puppy. I had to open my door slightly and follow the center line on the highway to get home.

I'll never know how I survived without causing an accident or being pulled over by the law. I suppose that proves that this DACBFM was intended to make it into adulthood. I may grow up someday.

On another occasion, when I had been out drinking, I bought large quart bottles of Colt 45 from a drive-through window at a black juke joint located on a dirt road out in the boondocks. The proprietor never asked for identification.

When I left the juke joint and was driving home on a dirt road, a set of headlights started getting closer to me from behind. They never tried to pass and I guess I panicked. I accelerated and I assumed I could outrun them in my four-cylinder Rambler.

Once I realized that it wasn't the law, I understood that it could only be J.C. I slowed down and drove straight home. I didn't park in front of the trailer but across the street at the cotton gin.

J.C. pulled up beside me, rolled down his window and just stared at me and shook his head. He never spoke of that incident to me for the rest of his life. I will never know if the thought that he'd been setting a poor example for us kids had ever crossed his mind, but I'm sure it had to have hit him hard that night.

The chase by J.C. ended here.

I sat in my car for several hours, crying as well as sobering up. I don't know everything that went through my mind that evening, but I do know that I seriously contemplated driving the little Rambler into the Mississippi River.

I dated several girls while attending Marianna High School, but only one made it to "three strikes and you're out." Her name was Cathy Sparks. Cathy was a tiny blonde with a pixie haircut. I really liked Cathy. Our dates would usually include a movie, a Frito Chili Pie from the DQ and finding a place to "park."

We both liked onions, so it was okay to go "parking" (making out) after a Frito Chili Pie smothered in raw onions. It's interesting to note, for just five dollars, we could put gas in the Rambler, go to a movie, and the DQ for Frito Chili Pie, and have change left over.

It broke my heart the night that Cathy asked when she was going to meet my parents. There was simply no way that I was going to take her to our 240 square foot trailer. I will never know if she ever understood why I broke up with her that night.

I can assure her and whoever is reading this, that it was not because of the onions! I suppose that I dated a half dozen girls other than Cathy while in Marianna, however they were all just "one date" and that was it.

One of my friends, John Kennedy, not "THE" JOHN KENNEDY, and I used to go camping at Bear Lake just a few miles from Marianna. We camped in an old military pup tent and slept in sleeping bags. We always roughed it, cooking over an open fire and fishing most of the day.

On one trip, we had friends bring us a case of beer, okay…maybe it was two cases of beer. It started raining in the late afternoon, so John and I got an early start on the beer.

It rained harder and harder as the night wore on and the more it rained, the more beer we drank. We were telling lies with the best of them. Late in the night, we saw headlights approaching our tent. It was my mom. Fortunately for us, she never got out of the car.

She honked her horn and yelled, "Do you want to pack up and go home?" We told her that we were fine and didn't want to leave. It's a good thing that she decided to leave us and come back the next day. Neither of us could have walked to the car, let alone break down camp and put it in the car.

John would eventually join the Marine Corps and was shot in the buttocks while in Vietnam, just like Forrest Gump. As far as I know, he lived a full life after the Corps. I only saw John one more time after I joined the Corps. I was on leave and while passing through Haynes on my way to California, we spent a little time together. By this time, he had gotten out of the Corps, and I had not yet gone to Vietnam.

In the summer before I left Marianna for good, several boys and I went to the levee on the Arkansas side of the Mississippi River, maybe five miles south of Memphis. We were just being stupid boys.

We were swimming in the Mississippi River and one of the boys had an inflatable air mattress. One of them bet me that I couldn't ride the air mattress all the way to the Mississippi side of the river. Yes, you guessed it, this stupid kid decided that it couldn't be that difficult.

So, I took the bet. Please keep in mind that we were all "buck-naked," how else can you go skinny dipping? Truth be known, none of us would spend our hard-earned money on something as mundane as a pair of swimming trunks.

Of course, there is an outside chance that we may have had a drink, or maybe two. The current was much stronger than I had imagined. I was maybe a hundred yards from the western bank when I realized that I didn't have a chance in Hell of getting to the eastern side of that river before the current started carrying me all the way to New Orleans.

I started paddling as hard as I could trying to get back to the western bank and I was making progress, even if it was at a snail's pace. About this time along comes the Mississippi Queen, an old paddle wheel driven river steamboat that was used to take tourists on the great Mississippi River out of Memphis.

The boat's crew apparently saw me, and the captain came as close as he could without flipping me over. I think the boat leaned heavily to the starboard side as all of the tourists and crew came to see the stupid kid on an air mattress with his white butt shining in the sun.

Once I knew that I couldn't avoid the humiliation, I started playing it for all it was worth. I patted my butt and waved at all the nice people.

Eventually, I made it back to the bank and the guys greeted me as a hero because of the way I literally showed my butt to those tourists. I still had to pay up on my lost bet. I often think that it is nothing short of a miracle that this DACBFM is still alive to tell the story.

    When I finished the twelfth grade in Marianna, I didn't wait for graduation. Our last day of class was on a Friday. The next day, I was on a Greyhound bus out of Memphis headed to Augusta, Georgia.
    I was eighteen years old by this time and my mother couldn't stop me. Just a point of interest, child support for both Boyd and me had terminated on my eighteenth birthday, December 6, 1966.

Class of 1967 Senior Portrait.

I had never been to Georgia, but I assumed that anywhere was better than where I was. My thinking was that maybe, just maybe, this would be like California. The bus trip from Memphis to Augusta was uneventful, except an old pervert tried to pick me up in a diner in Birmingham, Alabama.

Maybe that's part of the reason that I've never been a big fan of the state of Alabama. The pervert's pick-up line was "How large is your penis?" I was proud of my immediate response. I simply said, "Large, but not nearly as large as the knife in my back pocket!" He left the diner mumbling something about my mother's assumed profession.

As we drew closer to Augusta, I began to see signs related to Fort Gordon. Just west of Augusta, I could see a train depot that was apparently solely for the purpose of loading and unloading items intended for war. I don't know why, but this site has always been branded on my tiny brain.

When we pulled into the bus station in Augusta I was greeted by my dad, stepmom, Sharon, and her daughter Debra ("Dee-Dee" to me). We loaded my things into the car and headed to a mobile home park a short distance from Fort Gordon.

Once settled in, I started looking for a job. The only work, other than farm work, that I had ever done was working at restaurants or landscaping for Ernie's Trailer Park in California. I looked for other jobs but settled as a short-order cook for the Bonanza Steak house on Gordon Highway.

This may sound easy, but take my word for it, it's not. I had never cooked for anyone but family, but I was thrown into the fire, so to speak. I could cook a mean sirloin steak and was pretty good at making shrimp creole.

I attempted to enroll at Augusta Jr. College but discovered that I didn't have the required credits to even graduate from high school in Georgia. I needed only one credit, so I enrolled in Hephzibah High School in Hephzibah, Georgia. I only had to take one class and attend school for one hour a day for six weeks.

I would go to school around 9:00 A.M., leave after class and report to work at 11:00 A.M. I earned enough money to buy a 1958 Pontiac previously owned by the City of Augusta Fire Chief. The car was solid gray on the outside and had red and black vinyl seats. I was, indeed, "Styling!" The car would pass almost anything on the road except a gas station. I paid $0.24/gallon for gas and $5.00 each for re-capped tires.

I dated several girls while in Augusta; probably completely due to my learned habit, I only dated them once or twice. I dated a set of twins, who I couldn't tell one from the other. On one date, we were double dating to Six Flags over Georgia in Atlanta. We were halfway to Atlanta when I discovered that they had switched on me. We had fun anyway.

Most dates were either to the local drive-in movie theater or if you were brave, you would ask the girl if she wanted to go to the "submarine races" at Clarks Hill Lake. Now, everyone knows that if there was even such a thing as submarine races, you certainly wouldn't be able to see the darn things.

This was simply a ploy to get the girl to a remote parking site on the lake in order to make out. If the date said "Yes," you knew that it was going to be an interesting night or that this girl was incredibly naïve.

If she said "No," it was going to be a short date. However, if she said, "No," I could drop her at her home, drive five miles into South Carolina and sit down at a bar and drink to my heart's content, which I proceeded to do, more often than not. The legal age for drinking alcohol in South Carolina was eighteen.

The legal age for drinking of alcoholic beverages in Georgia was twenty-one.

In Vietnam, the military provided us with all the beer we could drink for only 10 cents a can. You could have as much as you wanted, but if you didn't like Schlitz or Pabst Blue Ribbon, you were out of luck. No one ever asked for my I.D. in Vietnam.

# 1968-1970 USMC, with One Year in Vietnam

When I had my nineteenth birthday in December 1967, I was still completely committed to finishing my last high school class in January 1968 and would re-apply to Augusta Jr. College.

Like I've previously said, I was raised to be patriotic, and at this time was convinced that service to our country was an honor and an expectation. My brother and father had already served in Vietnam and a good friend, James Earl Honeycutt, who played football with me in Marianna had enlisted in the Marine Corps.

The war was still going very strong; it dominated the news every evening. The news reporters always gave body counts, both Vietnamese and U.S. If you believed the news on television, you'd think that the outcome of that war was inevitable. We were obviously killing some serious numbers of people. That you kill doesn't necessarily mean that you're winning the conflict.

I suppose that I was under strong conviction to do something, so on Friday, February 9, 1968, I went to the U.S. Marine Corps recruiter's office on Gordon Highway in Augusta and enlisted. My thinking was that there would be ample time after Vietnam for college and of course, I'd have the VA school assistance. I had just celebrated my nineteenth birthday and technically had finished the twelfth grade in two states. I guess you could say that I was in the High School classes of 1967 as well as 1968. Both schools mailed my diplomas after I was in the Marine Corps.

The next day, my dad put me on a Greyhound bus from Augusta to Fort Jackson, South Carolina (located near the city of Columbia.) Fort Jackson was a U.S. Army base. However, it was apparently where they were giving physical exams for recruits as well as draftees for all branches of service.

On base at Fort Jackson, I spent my time in an old wooden barracks building left over from World War II and went through a series of tests. After completing all the tests and getting a few basic vaccinations, I was sent to another barracks building where they were holding the Marine recruits for shipping out to Parris Island, S.C. We were sworn in at Fort Jackson and soon loaded onto a bus heading to Parris Island.

We arrived at the front gate of Parris Island around 10:00 PM. on the evening of February 13, 1968. My first full day at Parris Island was Valentine's Day, February 14, 1968.

It was interesting to see and hear all the bravado and bragging on the bus ride down to Parris Island, however when the bus rolled through the front gate, you could have heard a pin drop. Most of us thought just because we had enlisted in the Marine Corps, we were now Marines. We were not!

The bus came to a stop in front of an old metal Quonset hut. This is a building constructed of corrugated metal shaped in a half circle. These buildings originated in the World War II era and were solid, easy to construct and almost impossible to cool or heat.

In front of the Quonset hut were sets of footprints painted yellow on the asphalt. The purpose of those footprints was to get the recruits familiar with the proper formation.

When the bus came to a stop, the front door opened and in walked our Senior Drill Instructor, Staff Sgt. J.E. Fitzgerald. SSgt. Fitzgerald would have been lucky if he weighed in at 150 pounds. But it was obvious from that first step onto the bus that he was THE MAN! At first, he spoke very softly, "Gentlemen, if you have any cigarettes, put them out, if you have any chewing gum in your "f'"ing" mouth, swallow it."

He continued, "Now you have three seconds to get the "f" off my goddamn bus and two of them are already gone." I think that the Drill Instructor's "cover" (it was never called a hat) blew off with the wind from all those brave boys exiting the bus, so much for bravado.

I'm glad my mother wasn't there to hear that speech. She surely would have wanted to wash my Drill Instructor's mouth out with soap!

After an hour or so, they marched/herded us into the Quonset hut and lined us up in front of racks (bunk beds). We were thinking that finally we would get some sleep, which was not to be. I don't know why they had racks in this building, we didn't use them all night. We would stand at attention for hours and as soon as you were feeling a little comfortable, the door would fly open, and a metal trash can would go flying down the middle of the squad bay.

Immediately following the trash can would come one or two drill instructors screaming obscenities that they had forgotten to yell the last time. This continued all night long. Once the sun came up, we were "dog tired." We had been up since early the previous morning, rode the bus for hours and stood at attention either outside or inside the squad bay all night. We were also mentally exhausted.

Next, they marched us to a medical area where we received a brand-new haircut, several vaccinations and drew our new uniforms and gear. We received our vaccinations before we changed from our civilian clothes and one of my tee shirt sleeves had a considerable amount of blood on it from the needles.

Once we were instructed to change clothes, we packed the civilian clothes into a box to be shipped home. I was told later that my stepmom freaked out when she received the bloody tee shirt.

The entire Marine training plan is to spend the first couple of weeks at boot camp breaking the recruit down to where he feels like he is the lowest scum on the face of God's green earth. As one drill instructor said, "You are so low, you could do a double backward flip off the edge of a dime," or "You could crawl under a snake's belly and would have to get on a step ladder to kiss the snake's butt."

If the recruit survives that mental torture, and most do, then his real training begins. It's at this point that they begin to mold Marines; you're not a Marine yet, but you are on your way. Normal recruit training for the Marine Corps is twelve weeks. Because of the Vietnam War, training at Parris Island and San Diego was reduced to only eight weeks.

Reveille was at 0400 (4 AM) each morning, and "lights out" was 2200 hours (10 PM). We trained from sunrise to sunset every day. Sundays were a little different, we went to religious services: protestant, Jewish or Catholic for an hour and then back to the barracks.

Sundays were much more laid back because all we did other than church/services, was close order drill, marching in formation and in unison, and calisthenics…a lot of calisthenics. We did get an hour every Sunday for personal time: writing letters home, polishing boots, etc. You did this while sitting on your footlocker.

Marine Corps boot camp consists mostly of medical examinations, basic equipment issue (including rifle), classification testing, strength testing, close order drill, and more close order drill, physical training and more physical training, manual of arms or how to handle and use your weapon, packing equipment, classes in weapons, chow (food) and more chow.

The food at Parris Island was surprisingly very good and there was lots of it. You spent hours with your drill instructors---please, don't ever call them "D.I.s." If you do, your butt is his and he would say, "Your ass is grass and I'm the GD lawn mower!"

We spent two of the eight weeks on the rifle range learning the M14 rifle inside and out. We had to be able to take it apart and put it back together in the dark. It's interesting to note that I loved my M14. However, once I left Parris Island, I never saw a M14 again. Everywhere else, we used the M16 rifle which could be fired as a single shot, a semi-automatic or fully automatic.

We all also got plenty of training on the M60 machine gun and the military-issued forty-five caliber automatic pistols.

The M60 was one "bad ass" weapon. We spent countless days in marksmanship training and a drill called "snapping in" which was a continuous practice of aiming at a dot on a sixty-gallon metal drum and dry firing (pulling the trigger with no ammunition in the weapon.)

This training was done for many hours before you were ever allowed to go to the range with live ammo. Record or qualifying day was where each recruit had a chance to show what he had learned.

We fired from a kneeling position, a prone or laying down position and a standing position. I was proud to qualify as a sharpshooter and I was the only one in our platoon to place five rounds in a sixteen-inch circle at three hundred yards with open sites.

The last thing that a shooter wanted to see was the dreaded "Maggie's drawers." This is where, should you miss the target altogether, you'd get a red flag waved back and forth in front of the target.

We had swimming classes, if the recruit didn't know how to swim, he would before he graduated from Parris Island. We had bayonet practice, hand-to-hand combat training, conditioning hikes with full field pack and weapons. We had the confidence course, for life training.

The "slide for life" consisted of a very tall tower with a two-inch diameter slide rope stretched from a platform on the high tower extending to the ground a few hundred feet away. The entire slide course contained a pond or mud puddle approximately 4 feet deep. Recruits had to cross the distance from the tower to solid ground using only their arms and legs and without falling in the water.

Finally, the gas chamber. We were marched into the gas chamber, a building that would barely hold a platoon of eighty men, with our gas masks on. Once inside, they would close the doors, turn on the tear gas and instruct everyone to remove their mask and sing the Marine Corps hymn.

Once you finished the singing, you would place your mask back on and clear it. When they opened the doors, everyone ran outside and most threw up their lunch.

Barracks

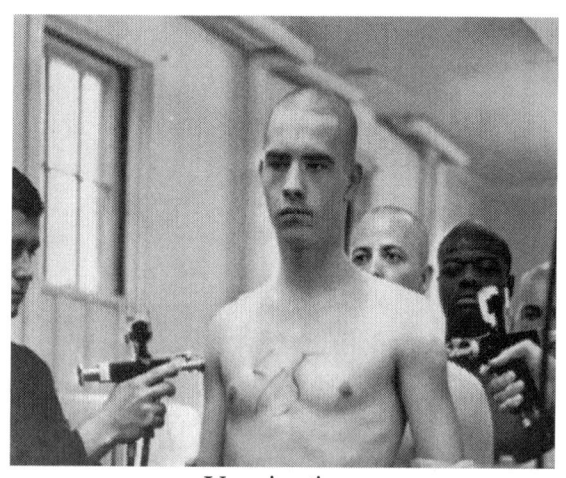

Vaccinations

Recruits had to go from the tower to the ground using their arms and legs without falling into the water.

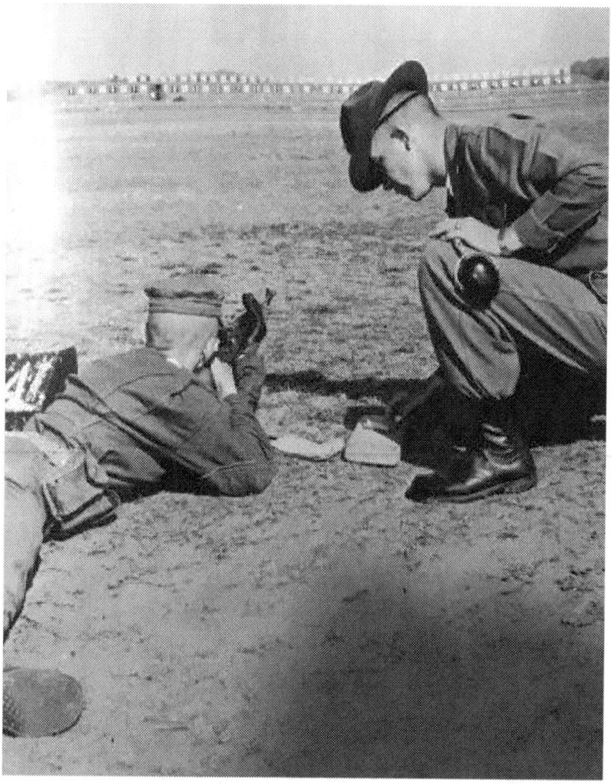

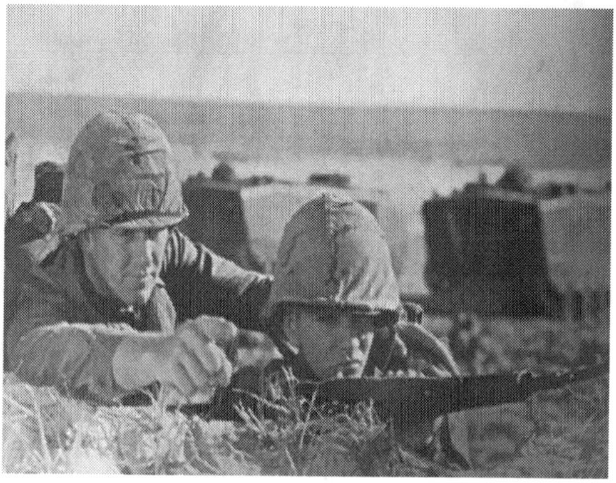

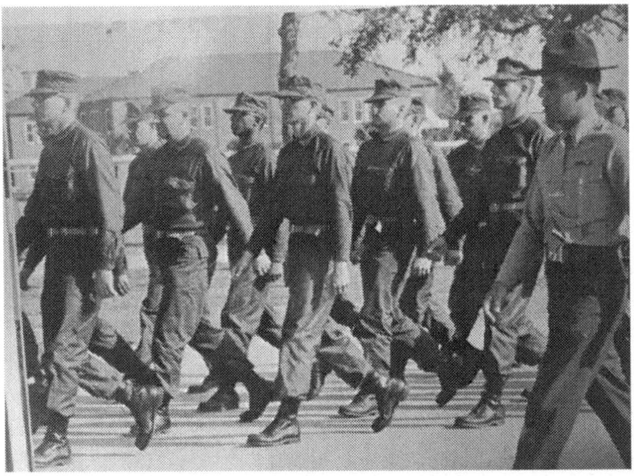

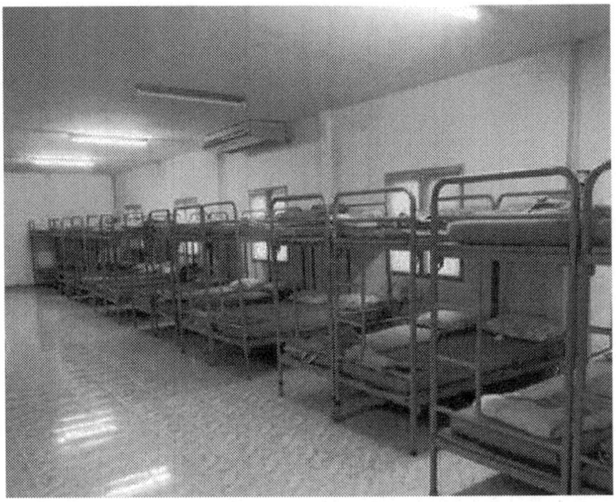

## My Rifle

THIS IS MY RIFLE. There are many like it but this one is mine. My rifle is my best friend. It is my life. I must master it as I master my life.

My rifle, without me is useless. Without my rifle, I am useless. I must fire my rifle true. I must shoot straighter than my enemy who is trying to kill me. I must shoot him before he shoots me. I will . . .

My rifle and myself know that what counts in this war is not the rounds we fire, the noise of our burst, nor the smoke we make. We know that it is the hits that count. We will hit . . .

My rifle is human, even as I, because it is my life. Thus, I will learn it as a brother. I will learn its weakness, its strength, its parts, its accessories, its sights, and its barrel. I will keep my rifle clean and ready, even as I am clean and ready. We will become part of each other.

We will . . .

Before God I swear this creed. My rifle and myself are the defenders of my country. We are the masters of our enemy. We are the saviors of my life.

So be it, until victory is America's and there is no enemy, but Peace!

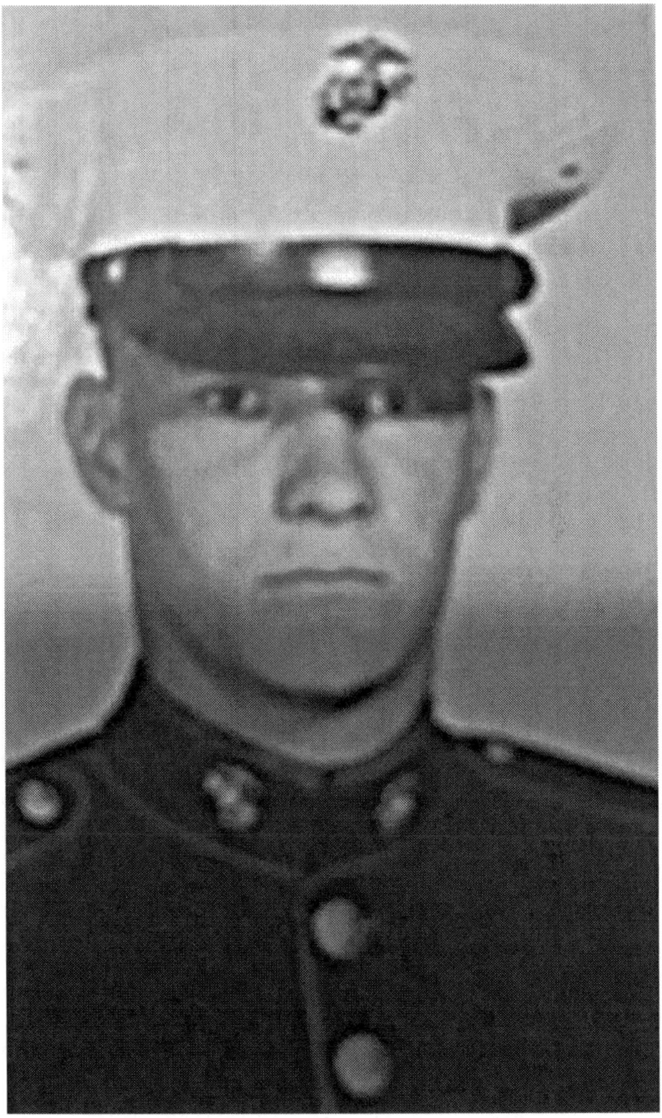

Just for the record, a recruit was NEVER to refer to his weapon as a "GUN!" I was never guilty of that serious error of judgement. However, I did observe the humiliation that one recruit had to endure after calling his weapon a "gun."

Once the drill instructor finished chewing him out up one side and down the other, he made the recruit strip down totally naked and stand in the middle of the squad bay on a footlocker.

For those who may not know what a squad bay and a footlocker are, the squad bay is the space between the two rows of bunk beds, approximately twenty feet wide. A footlocker is a lockable wooden box or trunk that one keeps all of their gear in. This box is stored at the foot of your rack, hence the name "footlocker."

The drill instructor then handed the recruit his M14 and made him stand in front of the entire platoon, approximately eighty men (boys), holding his M14 in one hand, repeating, "This is my weapon," and then his penis in the other and say, "This is my gun, my weapon is to kill with, and my gun is for fun!" Again, you simply cannot make this crap up!

After this single mistake and the humiliation of the one recruit, I never heard any other recruit call his weapon anything other than, "My weapon."

Every recruit had to pull mess duty for one week while at boot camp. For some reason, I drew mess duty at the WM (Women Marine) battalion. The only female recruit training facility in the Marine Corps is located at Parris Island, South Carolina.

I was doing a fantastic job of peeling potatoes and looking out a window at a brand-new batch of female recruits. These ladies had just gotten off the bus, they were still in civilian clothing, and most still had make-up on, smeared from tears as it may have been, and most were attractive.

The female drill instructor had a potty mouth that you simply wouldn't believe. She made the male drill instructors look like choir boys. After about an hour of humiliation and a quick meal, they marched off to their new home.

The next day, this same platoon of girls marched up to the chow hall again. This time the female recruits were dressed in their brand-new green utilities, all buttoned up to the very top buttonhole, no makeup, and all sporting their new pixie-type short haircuts. This potty-mouthed drill instructor was shouting orders, "left face, right face, etc."

The new ladies, all eighty of them, were not catching on to this close-order drill very well. The drill instructor stopped and raised her voice a few octaves and yelled, "Ladies, the next time I order 'right face,' all I want to hear is one hundred and sixty vagina lips slapping together at the exact same time!" Now, I cleaned this story up for "G-rated" audience readers. I was nineteen years old, and in my head, I said, "I really would like to hear that myself!"

I arrived on Parris Island late February 13, 1968. I started training the following day. Only a week after I started training, I received a letter from my mom letting me know that a friend and co-football player from Marianna, James Earl Honeycutt, was killed in action in Vietnam.

The directory for the Vietnam Veterans Memorial Wall in Washington lists the following:

"PFC–E2-Marine Corps-Regular, 20-years-old, arrived on December 22, 1967, the casualty was on February 17, 1968, in Quang Tri, South Vietnam, hostile, ground casualty, gun, small arms fire. The body was recovered, religion: Protestant."

James Earl had been in-country for only fifty-seven days. I had been on Parris Island for only three days.

Many years later Sgt. Major George Lyndsey called me at my Thomas & Hutton office. He had found my name taped to a piece of paper and attached to the Vietnam Veterans Memorial Wall over James Earl's name. He asked me if I was the one that the football team called "preacher boy" due to my stepfather being a preacher.

James Earl must have talked about some of our Marianna adventures. I have no idea how the paper got on the wall, nor do I know how Sgt. Major Lyndsey was able to track me down.

We talked for about an hour; the Sgt. Major was with James Earl when he was taken prisoner along with a few others. According to Sgt. Major, James Earl was safely onboard the extraction helicopter when his squad leader, a Lieutenant, was wounded, James Earl jumped off the safety of the helicopter and attempted to pull the Lieutenant on board. James Earl was shot several times and the helicopter had to take off before all were lost.

The Sgt. Major said that the North Vietnamese Army (NVA) pulled the lieutenant, James Earl, and a couple of others into the jungle. According to Sgt. Major, they came back with a full platoon of Marines a few days later to recover the bodies.

Apparently, James Earl and others had been captured and tortured before one of them was able to get free, obtain a weapon and kill many of their captors before being killed themselves. According to Sgt. Major Lyndsey, there were twenty-seven North Vietnamese Army (NVA) bodies near the dead Marines. The Marines either killed them all or the surviving NVA hauled tail before they, too, became casualties. The NVA didn't usually leave their dead behind.

James Earl received the Silver Star for attempting to save his wounded lieutenant before being killed himself; he is buried in the Forest City Arkansas Cemetery. He was only 20-years old.

I made myself a promise that should I ever be in danger of capture by the enemy, I'd save the last bullet for myself. Praise God! That never became an issue. The Vietcong or the NVA would rarely keep enlisted men as prisoners for very long. They would torture them to get as much information as possible before killing them in some grotesque way.

They would often leave their bodies where they were bound to be found by the Americans. What better way to destroy the morale of the troops than for them to see a mutilated corpse of a comrade in arms?

Obviously, the most important day in a Marine's life is the day that he/she graduates from boot camp. After this day, he/she will always be known as a Marine. Graduation day is a big deal in the life of a Marine and, in most cases, that of their families. Everyone in the platoon was excited about seeing their families, girlfriends, etc.

I did not expect to see anyone in my family and, I wasn't disappointed, no one showed up. I am not and do not intend any malice or disrespect toward my dad, however, I was extremely disappointed that he didn't come to the graduation.

He was in Augusta at the time, and that's only a little over one hundred miles away. The graduation was on a Friday. Even though I didn't have any family with whom to enjoy this day, it was the first day in nine weeks that we were allowed to roam the base without the entire training platoon.

I hung out with one other recruit who had no family to visit with. We went to the base theater to watch a movie, went to the PX to buy a few things, and simply enjoyed a little fresh air and freedom. The next morning, we boarded a bus heading to Camp Geiger, located inside Camp Lejeune, N.C. Camp Geiger was where we attended Advanced Infantry Training (AIT).

Once, near the finish of boot camp at Parris Island and once at Camp Geiger, I was offered Officer Training School (OTS). This was a three-month intense officer training school in Quantico, Virginia. Graduates were commissioned as second lieutenants and were considered "cannon fodder" in Vietnam.

These officers were referred to as "ninety-day wonders." If selected, you had to be willing to extend your commitment to six years. I turned it down both times, I had no desire to be cannon fodder, nor did I intend to serve any longer than for the purpose that I had enlisted in the first place, to serve my country in Vietnam.

Before being sent to Santa Anna, California, I took a couple of weeks leave. I went home to Augusta and shortly afterward met one of the longest lasting relationships of my unmarried life. Her name was Barbara Ione Mallette. Her sister was pregnant and married to a soldier who lived in the same trailer park as my parents.

She was born in Anchorage, Alaska. Her parents also owned a house in Seattle, Washington. She was between her junior and senior year at Linfield College in McMinnville, Oregon. Her father was a Methodist minister and pastored a church in Anchorage.

We enjoyed a few dates in Augusta, including a day on Clarks Hill Lake with my parents and my stepsister, Sharon. No submarine races were involved due to my family being present. When I left Augusta, I assumed that I'd never see Barbara again, just like most of the other girls/women in my life.

One thing led to another, and I would see her often during the course of the next year. We met in McMinnville, Oregon, Seattle, Washington and Anchorage, Alaska. I attended her graduation from Linfield College and met her parents.

It was obvious that her mom did not like the idea of her getting serious with a Marine. In her mother's mind, "A Marine was only good for two things, killing and chasing women." I can't say that I blame Barbara's mother; for the most part, her assessment of the Marines was spot-on.

When I left California on my way to Vietnam, we stopped for three hours in Anchorage for refueling. I called Barbara and she was at the airport within minutes. She was wearing tight jeans and a very fluffy Eskimo jacket with a full fur hoodie. She had waist length jet black hair.

Shortly before I left, she had asked me to come with her outside, get in her VW and we would drive to the Canadian border. She was sure that we could work things out. I'd be lying if I were to tell you that I didn't give a lot of thought to that idea.

As much as I cared, I could not go against all that I had been taught. I waved goodbye to her and left her crying in the terminal in Anchorage. We corresponded for several months, and she sent me a tape of Simon & Garfunkel's "Bridge Over Troubled Water," the number one song "back in the world."

I had a twenty-four inch by thirty-six-inch oil painting done of her by a Vietnamese artist. He painted it from a wallet size photograph that I had. It hung in my hooch until shortly before I "returned to the world."

A couple of months before I was to go home, I received a letter from Barbara letting me know that she was living with a guy in Oregon. This was 1970 and, for sure, "times were a-changin."

I never saw Barbara again although we did talk once over the phone after I'd been in Savannah, Georgia for maybe a year. I had given Barbara my Marine Corps ring prior to leaving for Vietnam. During our phone conversation, she offered to mail it back to me. I asked her to keep it. Who knows where it is today?

When I was "in-country" (Vietnam) for six months, I was given three options as to where I'd like to take my R&R (rest and recuperation). The options were Hong Kong, Tokyo, or Sydney, Australia. I put Sydney in all three places.

I assumed that I would be called into base operations and given Hell for my selections. Surprisingly, I wasn't.

I got to go to Sydney. I'll not go into all of the details, but I dated two different girls in Australia, one was an American and the other was an Australian nurse who worked in the Prince Henry Hospital in Sydney. We went to a ranch outside of town, ate huge steaks cooked on the open fire, rode horses in the moonlight and dodged kangaroos on the trail.

We went yachting in the Sydney harbor and often went dancing at a nightclub called The Coachman.

The Coachman was located in a high-rise building with a different theme on each floor. One evening, we were enjoying the band and dancing, not to mention the booze, when the band leader asked everyone to please sit down. We did as he asked and then he asked all the U.S. servicemen on R&R to please stand up, which we did. Not knowing what to expect next, we were surprised when he dedicated the next song to all the servicemen who were there. The name of the song was the old Irish classic, "Oh, Danny Boy."

When they were finished, there wasn't a dry eye in the building, and they had a standing ovation for more than five minutes. It was extremely moving; it also set the mood for the pretty ladies.

One evening as we were walking down the street late, a gentleman who was obviously under the influence approached us and said to me, "You blokes didn't accomplish a damn thing by going to the moon." I tried to explain that I had never gone to the moon, but he was convinced that I had. The conversation was pleasant enough, however, I had other things on my mind.

A pleasant sidebar to this encounter, just a few months earlier while at base operations at Chu Lai Republic of Vietnam, a C-130 landed and pulled in front of Base Ops and out walked none other than Bob Hope, Connie Francis, the Gold Diggers and most importantly, Neal Armstrong. It turned out that Base Operations had the only flushing toilet anywhere near the runway and they had stopped to take advantage of it.

While it was certainly exciting to see Bob Hope and all those pretty ladies, including Playboy's Miss June 1968, the fact that I met and shook hands with the first man to walk on the moon was one of the highlights of my life, with the exception of my family. You know I had to say that…all of my family is going to be reading this.

Other than the prospect of being killed in combat, one of the drudgeries of war is boredom. I've often heard it said that "War is 90% boredom and 10% absolute terror." One of the ways of combating the boredom while on the compound was flag football.

Some higher up in operations thought it would be healthy for the Marines to organize flag football teams. There would be competition between all the major bases in I-Corps.

Vietnam was divided into four separate areas of operation, they used the Roman numerals I, II, III, and IV Corps. I-Corps was the northernmost area of operation, and, but for a few exceptions was the responsibility of the Marine Corps. Instead of calling the area, "One Corps," it was referred to as "Eye Corps."

The genius who came up with this flag football idea decided that we would have competition among bases and eventually, the winning team would have a special R&R to Hong Kong. Everyone wanted to get that special vacation in Hong Kong, so the competition was brutal.

There were few rules and no officials. One day, we were locked in mortal combat on the gridiron (a red clay field) when suddenly mortar and 122 Russian rockets started pounding the base. They even hit one of the ammo dumps at the southern end of the compound.

We stopped playing football for a couple of

minutes. We weren't on perimeter duty and the action was a half a mile away, so we continued the game.

This was very important to all of us. A Lieutenant Colonel and I collided on a play, my tooth bit into his scalp and both of us were bleeding profusely. We were ordered to the sickbay for treatment, the Corpsmen thought we were wounded from the attack.

We got patched up and went straight back to the game. Unfortunately, we lost and didn't get to go to Hong Kong. (I'm sure we lost because I was in the sickbay… NOT!) Boys will be boys, no matter where they are.

Prior to my R&R in Australia, when I left the airport in Danang, Vietnam for the flight to Sydney, I had $1,600 in my pocket; that's equivalent to $12,000 in 2022 value. Now, that was a lot of money in 1970. When I got on the return flight from Sydney, I had six dollars and some change. I still have that today. That was the best small fortune that I've ever spent.

Shortly after I arrived in Vietnam, my dad received his orders for a second tour of duty in Vietnam. Dad could have asked to be excused from this tour because I was already in-country, and the military couldn't force two people from the same family to serve in a combat zone at the same time. Dad was a career Army soldier and he had already served a one-year tour at the same base as my brother, Boyd, in 1966.

He wasn't about to ask not to go this time. Shortly after he arrived in Danang, he was able to call me to let me know where he was stationed. He stayed at the air base in Danang for a few weeks and then he was transferred to the airbase at Phu Bai.

Phu Bai is located approximately sixty miles north of Danang and maybe one hundred and twenty miles north of where I was at Chu Lai. Phu Bai is only a couple of miles from Hue City where some of the fiercest battles occurred in February 1968 during the

Tet offensive.

On one occasion, dad was able to fly down to Chu Lai and we spent a couple of days together. We walked the beach at Chu Lai together and were under hostile fire the morning he and I were walking to the helicopter landing area where his ride was waiting.

On our way to the pickup area, a Russian-made 122 rocket landed in the middle of the dirt road maybe fifty yards in front of us. It didn't explode; it stuck in the ground like an Apache arrow and we simply walked around it, giving it a wide berth.

A few months later, at Christmas time, my commanding officer, who knew that my dad was "in-country," gave me a set of courier orders. The orders simply read to make my way to Phu Bai by any means possible and deliver a document to my dad. I hitched a ride on a C-130 sharing the cargo hold with several crates of chickens, one hog and maybe a dozen Vietnamese civilians.

We flew directly to Phu Bai and once we landed, it took me a while to find my dad. I finally found him in a supply tent sorting helicopter parts and placing them on shelves. In front of the tent was a long bar where the flight crews came to obtain new or replacement parts for aircraft. I was in full combat gear, camouflage utilities, flak jacket, two bandoliers of ammo, a forty-five caliber Marine Corps issue pistol, an M-16, and a steel helmet complete with camouflage.

Dad didn't recognize me. He looked me straight in the eyes and said, "How can I help you, Corporal?" I assume it was the shock effect; he wasn't expecting me. Once he realized who I was, he shook my hand just like a long-lost buddy, no hugs, etc. I handed him the orders that I was carrying. He opened the orders and read the message out loud, "Merry Christmas."

We spent three days together, including Christmas Day. We rode in a cattle car behind a truck to Hue City where we sat for four hours in the rain just to see the Bob Hope show. We ate Christmas dinner in the officer's mess at the request of the Commanding Officer. It was incredible. This was real food and the tables were covered with cloth tablecloths in an air-conditioned mess hall. I assume this was not the norm, but I was thrilled to participate.

Later that same day, my dad put me on an Army LOACH helicopter as the door gunner. The LOACH was a five-passenger helicopter used by all services as an observation helicopter and as an airborne jeep. The pilot was a red-haired, freckled faced nineteen-year-old.

Our job that day was to safely deliver a Major and a Captain to a firebase located a few miles west of Phu Bai, in the mountains. A fire base is basically the top of a mountain where it has been flattened in order to place two or three 105 Howitzer artillery pieces.

Fire bases were set up with an overlapping field of fire, when the good guys were in trouble, they would call for fire support. Almost always, there would be one or more fire bases that could fire upon "enemy positions" as they are called by the infantry.

The trip to the fire base was uneventful. However, we took heavy fire when landing and everyone on the fire base was firing into the jungle to suppress enemy fire. We were on the ground for less than thirty seconds and then we were gone. Now, that was a serious adrenaline rush.

Once we were clear of the fire base and on our way home, we came upon a fog bank close to the ground. It was Christmas Day, so the young pilot took the chopper down and we skimmed over the top of the fog with us both singing "Jingle Bells." You can take the young man "out of the world," but you can't take the world out of the young man. The pilot was only nineteen and I had just turned twenty-one a few short weeks earlier.

One would think that the trip to Firebase Mike, would be exciting enough for one Christmas Day, however, "Charlie" (the Vietcong) (VC) had other thoughts.

Dad's hooch (the building where he lived) was situated in a circle of hooches around a bunker. Three other men shared the hooch with my dad.

My dad's hooch maid and me, December 1969.

Like all military hooches in Vietnam, they were all constructed alike, plywood walls and partitions inside separating private areas. Dad had a single bed (rack) and I slept on the floor. Just outside dad's side of the hooch was a power pole. Early in the morning of December 26, 1969, we started taking fire, the first mortar hit the pole outside of dad's hooch and blew a large hole in the side of the building.

I don't know if it was the concussion from the exploding mortar round or something else, but I didn't wake up at first. I woke only after dad had me by the collar trying to drag me through the hole in his hooch. We both ran to the bunker and waited for the incoming to die down. The VC never made it through the wire; however, dad and I had a Christmas like no other before or after.

Me and Dad, December 26, 1969,
(Phu-Bai, Republic of Vietnam).

The following day, we were having lunch in the officer's mess and the CO asked me how I intended to get back to Chu Lai. I told him that I would go to the flight line and see if any of the aircraft were going my way and I'd jump on for the ride.

He told me that he had to get some required flight hours in the base U-21 (a twin engine, eight-person, Beechcraft) aircraft, so, if I didn't mind riding along, he'd take me back to Chu Lai.

Well, let's see, ride in a nice Beechcraft or a

C-130, I chose the U-21. Dad, the CO, and I climbed aboard, and I rode first class back to Chu Lai. The U-21 was generally used to carry high ranking officers up and down the coast of Vietnam.

So, when it pulled up in front of base operations at Chu Lai, naturally it got everyone's attention. The officer in charge of base operations came out to greet the dignitary on-board. He was likely disappointed to see a lowly Marine Corporal get off the plane and wave at the pilot and co-pilot as they taxied away. The co-pilot was my dad. All totaled, I rode in approximately eight different types of aircraft in Vietnam.

One of the things that I did as a volunteer while in Vietnam was to help a Navy Chaplain teach English at an orphanage in a small village just a few miles from the air base at Chu Lai. The Chaplin refused to carry a weapon, even when outside the wire.

I love Jesus but I like to have a backup plan. We would usually travel to the orphanage in the Chaplin's jeep and we would carry one other man. We always made a point of keeping in contact with base via radio and would never leave the base until well after sunup and would always be back on base at least one hour prior to dark, for our own safety. The other Marine and I were always armed, regardless of what the Chaplin chose to do.

On one trip to the orphanage, we came upon a South Vietnamese army patrol at a small bridge. They held us up for a while and being the curious person that I was, I had to go to the bridge to check things out. In the ditch and along the bank were several bodies of dead Viet Cong "Sappers."

Apparently, the VC were attempting to gain entrance to the airbase through the ditch or creek that the bridge crossed. Had the South Vietnamese Army patrol not intercepted them, the Viet Cong Sappers could have possibly gotten on the base and caused a lot of damage.

When teaching at the orphanage, we were, for the most part, simply repeating Vietnamese words in English and drawing on the chalkboard. The kids were unbelievably anxious to learn. Tutoring these kids was indeed a pleasure. One young boy loved to see me coming. He had found out that I'd lived near San Francisco for a while and every time he saw me coming, he'd run up to me and yell, "San Francisco Number One!" His other love was "Honda #1" Everything to him was #1, I don't know if he had a #2.

One day, while teaching, we heard gunshots outside the compound. The other Marine and I took positions at the windows on each side of the classroom, there was no glass. There was an eight-foot high fence maybe 50 yards away from the buildings that surrounded the complex. We held our positions for almost an hour, but the VC never made it over the wall. Some people have nothing but bad things to say about the South Vietnamese Army, but they saved our butts that day.

On another occasion after we had finished teaching, the Vietnamese Priest who oversaw the orphanage took us on a tour of the entire facility. We viewed where the kids slept, on wooden beds with no springs or mattresses, no sheets, no blankets. It was a very sad sight to see. Another important fact was that many of the kids were Amerasian, some obviously white and others black.

The Amerasian kids were segregated from the full- blooded Asians, and they were not allowed to participate in the school. Most, but not all of the Asian kids had been orphaned by the war, some carried scars from the actions that took their parents' lives.

It is so sad to think not only of the Vietnamese and American blood that was spilled in Vietnam, but of all the mixed blood kids who would have to spend their entire lives in a country that could not care less about them. That statement in no way diminishes the horrible cost that the Vietnamese people both South and North paid for an outcome that was inevitable from the onset.

After our tour of the facilities, the priest invited us to stay for dinner that evening. As we were talking to the priest, a woman was sitting on the concrete floor cutting up turnip greens (or at least it looked like turnip greens).

She was raking the stalks into a drain in the floor. While this was going on an elderly man, (Papasan) walked in the back door carrying a bundle of fur. The bundle of fur turned out to be a spider monkey, obviously we were going to have spider monkey and turnip greens for dinner.

I'm sure rice would be included as well. I can't tell you how happy I was when our Chaplin from base thanked the man but said that we had to be back on the airbase before dark for our own safety. Also, if the VC knew that we were in the orphanage after dark, and they would have certainly known, the lives of everyone in the orphanage would have been in danger. Remember, Charlie (VC) owned the night.

I did inquire as to how the Papasan caught the monkey. The Papasan would get a coconut and cut two holes in it, one at each end. One hole was a little larger than the other. The old man would slide a piece of rope through the small hole, tie a knot in it so it wouldn't slip out and tie the other end of the rope to a tree.

The trap would be located along a trail that monkeys were known to travel. He would then put several small pieces of tin foil from a gum wrapper near the trap and place the gum inside the coconut.

The monkey would smell the gum, see the wrappers, and stick his hand into the hole to get the gum. Once he closed his hand on the gum, he would not let it go and his fist would not slip back through the hole, even at the cost of getting his brains knocked out with a club. Simple, but it worked. There is a moral to that story, keep your hands away from where they don't belong. It could cost you your life.

While I have many memories of Vietnam, I refuse to glorify the war. Two events will stand out in my mind forever: one is when I first heard that Janice Joplin had passed away, I loved-me some J.J., and still love her music.

It was October 4 or 5, 1970, and I was on perimeter guard duty and was riding in the back of a six-by, this is a two-ton truck that can carry a lot of gear or at least a dozen fully equipped Marines We were outside the wire, on a red clay road near Chu Lai and a Marine with a transistor radio said, "Guys, you're not going to believe this, Janice Joplin is dead." I was devastated! I eventually got over it, but it took a lot of Scotch Whiskey.

I only did perimeter patrol for a week or so before the Marines pulled out. I was one of the last Marines to leave Chu Lai.

The other memory that stands out was when fire base Gator, about seven miles to the west of Chu Lai, was in the process of being overrun by the VC. It was late at night, and it was raining. The visibility was less than one mile but two men, one of them a Captain, got into an Apache attack helicopter and went to the fire base. When they arrived, the base was being overrun, they landed, picked up only one survivor of the attack and he was seriously injured.

The copilot placed the wounded man in his seat, the chopper only had two seats. The copilot then straddled the rocket pod mounted on the side of the Apache and rode it the seven miles back to Chu Lai in the rain. Now, that took serious courage. The man that they rescued from the fire base was the only survivor.

On August 1, 1970, not long before I left Vietnam, I was ordered to report to Base Operations. Being a good Marine, I did as I was ordered. When I arrived, there were five other men waiting outside and I was ordered to fall in with these men.

I hadn't a clue what was happening, when the CO came out and read off six identical Combat Promotions, I was meritoriously promoted to Sergeant, E-5 via a combat promotion. The ceremony was short and sweet, the CO made an about face and marched back into his hooch. I folded the piece of paper and placed it in my breast pocket. That combat promotion is displayed in my study today and the folds can still be seen where I folded it to go in my pocket.

In early October 1970, I would board a 707 in Danang bound for Okinawa. I have never looked back, and I will never visit Vietnam again.

My honorable discharge from the

United States Marine Corps, February 12, 1974.

My Combat Promotion issued on August 1, 1970.

It was pouring rain in Danang as I was waiting under a metal roof to board the 707 bound for Okinawa. A Vietnamese man, again you can't make this crap up, approached me wearing a trench coat.

At first, I was a little concerned as to what his intentions were. After all, it would have been a shame to die in the airport awaiting departure from Vietnam. Then he opened the coat to reveal hundreds of pieces of jewelry, watches, etc.

He was obviously selling these items that he purchased from the black market. I assumed that the jewelry items were knock offs, but one got my attention. It was a 14-carat gold ring, with two diamonds mounted on each side of a beautiful star sapphire.

The man wanted $150 U.S. dollars for the ring. I only had $75 in what we referred to as "funny money." This was U.S. military scrip that was only good in Vietnam. These Military Payment Certificates (MPC) were created in an effort to curb black-market activities. I was on my way out of country, so the scrip was soon going to be useless to me.

I offered him the $75 dollars and after a little haggling, he accepted it.

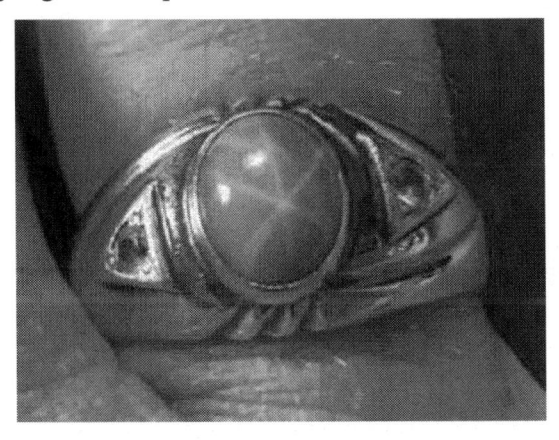

I assumed that I had simply thrown away my money, however, a few weeks later while staying with friends in Long Beach, California, I went to a local jeweler and asked for an appraisal. The jeweler offered me $750 on the spot. I turned him down and I still have and love my "last night in Vietnam ring."

I spent three days on Okinawa where we went through a thorough debriefing prior to being allowed "back in the world." In case I didn't mention it earlier, the phrase "back in the world" is how we Marines, in Vietnam, referred to back home in the U.S.A. We also picked up our stateside uniforms and civilian clothes which we stored on our way to Vietnam.

An interesting story that needs to be told is that while in Vietnam, base perimeters were always lit at night by flares. These flares could be dropped from aircraft, shot from mortar tubes or even from artillery. Once opened, all of the flares were gently swinging by small parachutes for the purpose of lighting the base perimeter.

The intent of the flares was two-fold: 1) To discourage Charlie (the Americans referred to the Viet Cong as Victor Charlie, VC, or simply Charlie) from attacking and, 2) To allow the Marines to see the VC should they be bold enough to attempt to advance on the base.

For all intents and purposes "Charlie" referred to all communist forces---both Viet Cong and North Vietnamese.

The point being that the base perimeter was always lit. As we landed on Okinawa at night, on the bus ride from the air base to our assigned barracks, one of the first things that I noticed was that the flares weren't moving…they were streetlights. It's amazing how the human brain can become accustomed to almost anything.

Prior to leaving Vietnam, I was given the option of retraining once stateside or getting an early release from my enlistment due to my service in Vietnam. I only enlisted in the Marine Corps to serve my country in Vietnam; I had done that.

So, I opted for the early release. I had no intention of becoming a career military man and there was nothing left for me to do. I was separated from active duty in the recruit depot in San Diego, California. My total service to the Marine Corps was two years, seven months, and twenty-seven days of active duty.

The remainder of my six-year enlistment was spent in the inactive Marine Corps reserve, no meetings, no drills, etc. I received my Honorable Discharge on February 12, 1974.

I was separated from active-duty October 09, 1970, at the Marine Corps Recruit Depot, San Diego, California. Shortly after receiving my separation orders, a friend who was stationed in Vietnam with me, Norman, and I went to the Base Exchange (PX), to purchase a few articles of civilian clothes.

I also purchased a backpack and a jacket. We tossed all our military clothes before leaving the base. Norman and I hitched rides north from San Diego to Long Beach. I had Marine Corps buddies who lived in Long Beach and were stationed at the Santa Anna, Marine Corps Air Station.

We spent a couple of days catching up and just blowing off pent-up steam. It was strange trying to enjoy some good times with friends that you had known prior to Vietnam and who themselves had never been to Vietnam.

They loved to tell you exactly what we should do to win the war. All I could do was smile and walk away. Little did they know wars like that can't be won, they can only be endured.

After a couple of days enjoying the beach, babes, and fun of Long Beach, Norman and I hit the road, hitching rides all the way to Seattle.

Somewhere north of San Francisco, we were picked up by a VW van driven by two very long haired and high hippies. The van was multi-colored on the outside and totally decked out on the inside with insane posters, bags of weed, pipe, etc.

These guys were legit 1970 hippies. We rode with these guys all the way to the Oregon and Washington state lines. I believe that all these guys ate were chocolate brownies (In 2024, they would be known as "edibles.")

I'll have to admit that I enjoyed a few myself. Yes, they were packed with weed (marijuana), and I've never slept better in my life. Two interesting events occurred while we were riding with these two guys.

First, we were following behind this VW bug (the original Volkswagen that looked like Herby) and a deer jumped out in front of and was hit by the VW. Our driver pulled over behind the VW bug and we got out to see if we could help.

Two very pretty young ladies, also hippies, in the VW bug were both clearly shaken up from the event. Norman and I went to drag the deer out of the road, and we discovered that it wasn't dead. The poor deer had one broken back leg, a broken hip and a couple of ribs protruding from its side. I pulled my trusty hunting knife from its scabbard attached to my backpack and cut the deer's throat, thus putting it out of its misery.

The girls went insane. They yelled, "You animal, we could have taken it to a veterinarian!" The two dudes that we were riding with simply said, "WOW!"

The deer would not have lived, regardless of what they or we may have done. I did the most humane thing that could have been done. Needless to say, we didn't make any points with the two ladies.

Norman and I pulled the deer carcass to the ditch, and we went on our way in the hippie van. I think we left the two young ladies having some sort of last rights for the deer and the two dudes we were riding with were afraid to not take us further. As we got back in the van, one of the guys just kept saying, "Wow, dude, that was gnarly!"

The second memorable event while riding with these two dudes was our last night on the road. These guys would stop in road-side parks and spend the night in their van. Norman and I slept in our sleeping bags outside under the stars. Our last night was cold and we zipped our sleeping bags all the way up and slid our heads as deep inside as possible.

During the night, I began to feel uncomfortable, unable to breath without effort. I unzipped my sleeping bag and threw it back only to find over a foot of snow had fallen during the night. Norman appeared to be sleeping very well or maybe he was dead, so I left him alone. I pulled my sleeping bag under a picnic table and climbed back inside.

The next morning, after a hearty breakfast of brownies, and as we came within an hour or so of Seattle, our two new friends dropped us off. They didn't even leave us any brownies for the road. How rude!

We got one more ride all the way into Seattle, where I called my brother, Boyd, and he came and picked us up. I had planned to purchase a new car while in Seattle, drive it to Augusta with stops in Arkansas to see my mother and New Orleans, Louisiana, Norman's hometown.

Boyd had talked me into buying a Mazda. I had never even heard of the Mazda brand. I bought one anyway. They were supposed to be very economical and reliable vehicles. I wanted both.

The dealership asked that I not take the car across the country until they could do a 600-mile checkup. So, Norman and I toured Seattle, Tacoma, Victoria, British Columbia, Canada as well as Portland, Oregon.

We visited with Boyd and his wife, Linda, as well as with Billie Steve and his wife, Paula. Just for the record, and in case I haven't previously introduced these people, Boyd is my only 100% full blooded brother, Linda was Boyd's wife and Billie Steve is my stepbrother and his wife is Paula. Boyd and Billie Steve both lived in Seattle at this time.

A couple of weeks passed, and I had the 600-mile checkup done on the new little car, it checked out, and we were good to go. Billie Steve had given me a Siberian Husky by the name of Smoky. Norman, Smoky, and I headed across the country.

On our trip Norman and I visited Yellowstone, Mt. Rushmore, the Badlands of South Dakota, and the Little Bighorn battle site, on our way to visit my mom in Arkansas. The seats in the Mazda would lean back almost all the way so we were able to sleep well in our sleeping bags with Smoky in the middle. We spent the night in the parking lot of Old Faithful as well as Mt. Rushmore. Most of the trip was over snow covered roads, which the Mazda handled very well, given that it was not four-wheel drive.

Before long, we pulled up in front of the trailer that mom was living in near the church in Arkansas. Immediately, I knew that something was wrong when Mom came out to meet us. This was how I learned that J.C. had left mom.

This caught me off guard, however, I can't say that it surprised me. I assume that I wasn't informed earlier because Mom simply didn't want me to worry while I was in Vietnam.

We spent a couple of days visiting with Mom, Deb, and Jay before we were off to New Orleans.

I enjoyed meeting Norman's family, especially his mom. She was Cajun to the nth degree. I could hardly understand a word she said, however, that woman could cook! I stayed with them a little over a week before heading back north to check on Mom, Deb, and Jay. I spent one night with Mom before heading east to Memphis to visit relatives and eventually on to Augusta.

Arriving at my parent's place in Harlem, Georgia, about twenty miles west of Augusta, is where the lifelong bonding event occurred between my sister Sharon and myself. Her running to meet me, crying and telling me how much that she'd prayed for me was the glue that formed that lasting relationship.

My plan was to spend a week or so visiting my dad and stepmother before heading back to Seattle to start my life. I had planned on settling down either in Seattle or Sydney, Australia. Dad had just returned from Vietnam and the Army was going to move him from Fort Gordon in Augusta, Georgia to Hunter Army Airfield in Savannah, Georgia.

Dad asked me if I would stay long enough to help move him and mom to Savannah. History was one of my favorite subjects in school and Savannah was one of the most historic cities in the U.S., so I agreed. Once I arrived in Savannah and had time to explore, I fell in love with the city. Two years later Dad was transferred to Fort Rucker, Alabama and I was still in Savannah.

Within a couple of months of arriving in Savannah, I was able to rent a fully furnished garage apartment that belonged to Colonel Logan, a former Chatham County Engineer. I paid $75 a month which included all utilities. I did not have a phone nor the money to have one installed.

Yes, you had to have them installed in those days, they didn't fit in your pocket. I was in luck though, Mrs. Logan never locked her back door and there was a phone on the wall just inside the back door. She told me to use it anytime I wanted.

I enrolled in Armstrong State College, located at the South end of Abercorn Street. Armstrong was a very small state college at the time, with no dormitories, etc. Most of the students were local and lived at home. While attending classes at Armstrong, I had to get part-time jobs to make ends meet.

I went to work for a company called Abbot Temporary Employment Services. The beauty of working for Abbot was they would call me one day to see if I could work the following day or sometimes even that night, if I could I'd agree, and if I couldn't, I didn't have to. One day Abbot called me and said that they had a large job that was going to take approximately three months.

At first, I told them that I couldn't commit to full time for three months, however after the little incident in math class, I agreed to work only on this project until its completion. I was taking a sabbatical from school.

The project was working on a survey crew for a local company, Thomas & Hutton Engineering (T&H). The project was to produce a topographic map of Elba Island. Elba is an island in the Savannah River, located approximately eight miles down the Savannah River from the City Hall of Savannah. At this time, the only way to get to Elba was by boat.

Thomas & Hutton's office was located on Factor's Walk with a rear garage door on River Street. At the time, River Street had not been renovated, it was nothing more than rat infested falling down wharfs and warehouses. Thomas & Hutton had rented a thirty-foot cabin cruiser that they tied up behind City Hall. We would meet on River Street, get on the boat, and ride the forty-five or so minutes to Elba.

Once we anchored in the back-river behind Elba, we would load all the equipment on board a wooden bateau and row it to the shore. In the afternoon we'd reverse the process and return to City Hall. The crew chief for this little adventure was none other than Andrew J. Patterson, affectionately known as "A.J. Squared Away."

Andrew, or "Pat" as most people called him, was the first black survey crew chief in southeast

Georgia. Pat had worked for many years for a white crew chief, Billy Itell. Billy wore khaki pants, khaki shirts and always had at least two pens in his shirt pocket; he also had a small six-inch engineer's scale and slide rule. Pat was a spitting image of Billy, only Pat was black.

The project that we were given, or I should say that Pat was given, was to manually cut over seventy-five miles of survey line, basically a straight cleared line from the Back River to the Savannah River. These lines would be used to obtain horizontal and vertical data so that the engineers could produce an accurate topographic survey of the entire island.

When I arrived on Elba Island, I knew nothing about land surveying or civil engineering. I did find that this was something that I really enjoyed doing, at least in concept. The math problems that I'd had so many issues with in school were beginning to evolve into something that I could see, feel, and could make some sense of when actually applying them in a real-world situation.

Let's go back to the issues that I had at Armstrong with math. Math was never my strong suit. I enjoyed math until it advanced to geometry and trigonometry, not to mention calculus. I was taking math 101, a remedial course to prepare me for college level math.

I had a female professor, whose name I will not reveal, and I should have known that I was in serious trouble when I noticed that this lady didn't shave any part of her body, not her legs, her armpits, etc. I have no firsthand knowledge of other parts.

She wasn't that unattractive except for the hair. She didn't wear makeup or do anything with her hair other than let it hang straight. She could have made pigtails with the hair in her armpits. I guess you can see by now that she was a hippie, liberal, etc.

She and I had nothing in common. She had red hair and freckles all over her face and body. I had no issues with any of this until, one day in class I raised my hand like a good little boy (student) and the professor walked over to me and said, "Mr. Young, you're a Vietnam veteran, aren't you?"

I didn't expect anything out of the ordinary, so I answered, "Yes, Ma'am, I am." She pointedly said, "Mr. Young, you'll never pass a class under me." I wanted to say, "Who the Hell would want to be under you?" I didn't; I simply picked up my crap and walked out.

I did go back to take several more classes at Armstrong College. I eventually finished at Savannah State, a traditionally all black college. I fit in perfectly at SSU and never felt uncomfortable and, I might add, that I was always treated with respect.

Eventually, I would also spend time taking classes in eight different colleges, including a two-year program from "International Correspondence Schools" (ICS) for civil engineering technology.

I also attended a two-week course for real estate law at Winthrop College, located in Rock Hill, South Carolina. Winthrop College was originally a women's college. However, by the mid-1980s it had become co-ed.

This school was offering a two-week, eighty-hour course in real estate law. It was designed primarily for paralegals, title researchers, and Land Surveyors. The legal classes were part of the requirements to complete my education and allow me to take (and successfully pass) the Professional Land Surveyors exam for the State of South Carolina.

An interesting story concerning Andrew J. Paterson: Pat was a very hard worker. He was loyal to his crew chief and to Thomas & Hutton Engineering Co. Pat learned everything that he knew from Billy

Itell, the way that he dressed and the way that he performed his surveys.

Pat was a good man with a good heart. He tried to mentor employees who worked under him. For the most part, Pat's crew consisted of Leroy Reeves, Lamon Green, Joe Baker, and me (all African American men, except for me).

I enjoyed working with Pat. He taught me an enormous amount concerning the field aspects of land surveying. Pat was apparently a hell-raiser during his younger days, whiskey, women, etc. When Pat was in his forties, he was working on a survey with Billy Itel, and he was asked to climb a fence that surrounded an electric substation.

Apparently, Billy needed an elevation inside the fenced area. Shortly after Pat climbed the fence (they fence these things for a reason), he was struck by a bolt of electricity from the transformer. It struck him in the head and knocked him out. Billy had to get the power company to turn off the power to the substation so that Pat could be retrieved.

Pat recovered from this event, and he never drank another drop of alcohol or chased women again, or so he said. Shortly after this event, he surrendered to the ministry. Sometimes knowing God's will takes a shocking situation. Pat had two distinct holes in his head where the electric current entered and exited his body.

Surprisingly enough, the two holes were located where horns would have been had he been the devil. Pat was not the devil.

Pat is the reason that I stayed in Savannah and stayed with Thomas & Hutton Engineering Co. One day, while working on Pat's crew, I was talking to him about my friend Norman and our plans to move to Sydney, Australia. Norman was working on the plan for us to sign up to work our way to Australia on a cattle freighter. The trip would take 29 days on a cattle freighter from San Francisco to Sydney. We would be paid handsomely for our services. The Australian government would set us up with jobs on a cattle ranch.

Apparently, Australia was looking for a few good men to boost their economy. When I considered my good fortune during my seven-day R&R trip to Australia, I thought this might be a good start to a lifelong adventure.

When I shared my plans with Pat, he was mortified. He sat me down and started talking about my potential career at Thomas & Hutton, etc. Please remember that I'd only been working with T&H for less than two months.

Pat and I had developed a lifelong friendship on the Elba Island project. I was only twenty-two years old. Over the following nine months, I worked with several crew chiefs including Billy Itel, Buzzy Gavin, and Andrew "Pat" Patterson. By this time, I was certain about what I wanted to do with the rest of my life, and I began taking night classes at Armstrong College.

Pat said, "Boyce, you don't need to do that (Move to Australia). You stay with T&H. You'll be a partner someday." I thought, "This black man is definitely crazy ("Cray- Cray")." I knew absolutely nothing about land surveying or civil engineering.

For whatever reason, I stayed, and Pat turned out to be clairvoyant. I eventually became a licensed, Professional Land Surveyor in multiple states with a degree in Civil Engineering Technology from Savannah State College and yes, a partner at Thomas & Hutton Engineering Company. While reliving this story, I can't help but recall the bus trip from Memphis to San Francisco in 1964.

Pat thought that Dianne Herrington walked on water. Just to clarify this, she didn't and to this day I've not seen her do so. Dianne eventually became my wife and Andrew J. Patterson (also known as "A.J. Squared Away") was the preacher who performed the service.

The wedding was performed at Calvary Baptist Temple, one of the largest, traditionally white Baptist churches in Savannah, Georgia.

Rev. and Mrs. Andrew J. Patterson.

During the service, Pat turned and said, "Does anyone here have any objections to this marriage?" And then he added, "And, if you do, I had better not hear a word from any of you. An interesting sidebar, Calvary Baptist eventually called a black preacher to be their pastor.

Pat eventually worked as a crew chief under me when I managed all the surveying and mapping operations for Thomas & Hutton.

Just a few days before Pat passed away, a mutual friend, Mike Eckman, and I visited Pat at his home on his deathbed. Pat was a friend and probably the main reason that I stayed in Savannah and with Thomas & Hutton.

Pat's wife asked me to say a few words at Pat's funeral. I agreed and to the best of my knowledge, I was upbeat and positive. The funeral was held in an old traditionally black church in downtown Savannah, where Martin Luther King, Jr. once spoke in the 1960's.

If you wanted a survey project done fast, you didn't send Pat. If you wanted it done right, Pat was your man. I used to ask him how he was doing on a project and his patented response was, "Just one more day boss." It never happened in just one more day. At his funeral I told his wife and family that to deal with this loss, they had to take it just one more day at a time. I loved this man called Andrew J. Patterson, Pat, Preacher, and friend.

Backing up a little, when the project on Elba Island was completed, I was called into the office of Wright Powers, Sr. Wright was the head of the surveying department at Thomas & Hutton. Wright was a WWII veteran; he served with an engineering battalion in Europe as a cartographer. His rank was captain. He offered me a full-time job.

I wasn't sure that I wanted to do that, but I agreed, and he started me at $1.25 per hour. I thought I had died and gone to heaven. After one month on the job, Wright called me back into his office and told me that he was going to increase my salary if I'd stay. He said, "Please don't tell anyone because we normally only give $0.10 per hour raises but we're prepared to offer you a $0.50/hour increase if you will continue with T&H."

That brought my hourly salary to $1.75, a fortune in my eyes, and I agreed. I soon began taking night classes with a specific goal of becoming a civil engineer/land surveyor. Eight years later, I had an equivalent of a civil engineering technology degree from Savannah State College. I didn't do it in the conventional way, but I had proven my dear mother wrong.

People like us do go to college and we do complete our studies to become certified and successful in whatever roles we desire. It just takes determination and "stick-to-it-ness." If you are a Young descendant, you have both of those in your genes.

During the first three years of my career at T&H, I worked in the field on a survey crew. The first year I was an instrument man, meaning that I operated the transit, level, etc. The next two years I was a crew chief.

After this, I was asked if I would consider being an inspector for construction projects that T&H designed. I agreed and worked with Wright Powers, Sr. as an inspector. After Wright left T&H, I became the head inspector.

I continued to serve in this capacity for a total of seven years. I worked primarily for Frank Vreeland George (T&H President and CEO as well as a retired Lt. Col. in the USMC) and with Steve Roach (a friend and eventually a partner with T&H). My responsibilities gradually grew into the design of projects.

Most of my projects were storm drainage, paving, grading and drainage. I also designed water distribution projects and wastewater collection systems. I spent several years doing design work. The unique thing about the projects that I designed was that I personally supervised the survey data collection, the plotting of this data, the design, and drafting of the final plans.

I also wrote the design specifications for each project. After the design, I helped the client prepare bid packages for the contractors and I also supervised the construction. This was a dream come true; I had become a real design engineer.

In the mid-1980's, Mr. George saw the handwriting on the proverbial wall. I didn't have a civil engineering license and without going back to school and obtaining a four-year civil engineering degree, I would not make it much further in the company.

Mr. George asked me if I'd consider taking the job of managing all T&H's surveying operations. At first, I didn't really want to do that because I was seriously enjoying what I was doing and simply didn't want to let it go.

After a lot of thought and heartfelt fear of the unknown, I realized that Mr. George was right. If I were to advance in the company, I needed to focus on what my professional license would legally allow me to do. I approached Mr. George with the concept of me taking command of the Surveying & Mapping department while I continued to do design work.

I was very optimistic that I could do both. After struggling with a few design projects as well as managing the survey department, it became obvious that no one could do both. The Thomas & Hutton Engineering Company was growing, and we had three offices: Savannah, Charleston and Myrtle Beach, S.C.

I finally gave up the design responsibilities and focused entirely on Surveying and Mapping. Mr. George was right, had I not given up the design work, I'm sure that I never would have become a partner.

The project that I was most proud of was when Steve Roach and I decided that we could get into the LIDAR (light detection and ranging) business. LIDAR is a method of obtaining three-dimensional topographic data using an aircraft mounted laser, GPS, and reference points on the ground to obtain very accurate topographic data over large areas.

We partnered with a company out of Jackson, Mississippi. This company was already experimenting with LIDAR but not on large tracts of land. We contracted with six local clients to provide LIDAR topographic maps of tracts ranging from four hundred to six hundred acres.

Our agreements with these six clients were that if they weren't happy with the final product, they didn't have to pay for it. This was a huge (and potentially very expensive) gamble for us.

T&H provided all the ground reference points for the X, Y & Z coordinates, our partners from Jackson provided the plane, laser, and raw data. Once the data had been collected, processed, and proofed, we provided the topographic maps to our clients. All six clients were thrilled with the product and paid us our asking fee.

Shortly after we finished these projects, Chatham County, Georgia put out for bids to provide a two-foot interval accurate topography survey of the entire county. We placed a winning bid of over eight million dollars, and we got the project.

Once again, we partnered with the company out of Jackson, Mississippi. We finished the project months ahead of schedule and to the satisfaction of the county. We made one of the largest profits, percentagewise, up to that date in the company's history.

Shortly after this project was completed, Thomas & Hutton was selected to design a stormwater collection system for Chatham County, including designing several multi-million dollar storm water pumping stations. The accuracy of the topographic data obtained using LIDAR technology saved over three million dollars in construction costs for the county on that project alone.

## 1970-PRESENT

After one year of trying to do both design and surveying, and struggling with a particularly difficult design project, I gave up on design. I didn't want to stop designing. However, my education and licenses were in Land Surveying, not engineering.

Eventually, as a result of Mr. George's encouragement, I was asked to be a partner with Thomas & Hutton Engineering Co. and took on the responsibility of Director of Surveying for the company.

We had four offices at that time and opened the fifth after I became Director. When I retired from Thomas & Hutton Engineering Co. in 2011, we had five offices. Thomas & Hutton now has twelve office locations in four states. Things certainly have changed since I started working with T&H in 1971 when we had only one office and twenty-seven people.

I would never have enjoyed the benefits of being a partner in such a prestigious engineering company and having the privilege of working on that level with highly qualified co-workers had it not been for a lot of great people along the way.

Had Andrew "Pat" J. Patterson not forcefully encouraged me to let go of my plans to move to Australia, had Steve Roach not tutored me in math, and, most of all, if Mr. George had not talked me into doing something that I didn't want to do, who knows what the end of this story would have looked like.

I consider myself one of the most blessed and fortunate man having lived and having enjoyed such profound relationships and experiences that, during my childhood, one could have never dreamed possible.

I also think that had it not been for my grandparents teaching me the importance of hard work, these dreams would have never come to fruition. If there is a principle to be learned from my life, it's that you can and should learn from all of life's experiences, good and/or bad.

I retired from Thomas & Hutton Engineering Company June 24, 2011, after forty years. The retirement party was incredible and still brings tears to my eyes. I'm still looking for exactly what I'm going to do once I grow up.

For over ten years I had the privilege of being a member of the Rotary Club of Savannah, West. I served as President the year our club received the Rotary Club of the Year Award in the State of Georgia. The year that I was President we were able to form a sister club with the Rotary Club of Lahore, Pakistan and I also received the Rotarian of the Year award for the state of Georgia.

My commitment to Rotary ended a couple of years after my retirement only because I'd gotten interested in projects in Haiti and I simply couldn't afford both. I was funding my own trips to Haiti and my

Rotary Club expenses.

I made my first trip to Haiti with my daughter Kimberly in 2012 and eventually traveled to Haiti a dozen or so times. I taught school, did surveys, helped with hurricane relief and just about anything I could find that the missionaries would allow me to do.

I learned to love the Haitian people and the simplicity of the way they live. Most are very loving and caring people, unfortunately there are always a few that give the whole nation a bad name.

The stories I could tell concerning Haiti would take volumes and they still wouldn't begin to communicate why many volunteers have dedicated their entire lives to this country. I can think of nothing else that's given me more satisfaction and self-worth than the time I've spent in the Caribbean country of Haiti. I've never experienced a closer spiritual connection than time spent in Haiti.

I don't want to go into much detail concerning my involvement in Haiti except for a couple of stories that may give the reader a little comfort in a dark world. On my first trip to Haiti, I went with my daughter, Kimberly. She was taking her daughter who was thirteen at the time. This was Kaitlyn's first trip, and, in my ignorance, I was going to be a bodyguard for my granddaughter.

I had no idea what I was going to do, I had never been on a mission trip and felt poorly qualified to do any of what was planned. Kimberly and Kevin (her husband) were conducting a Vacation Bible School for the kids in Jubilee, a very poor refugee village just on the outskirts of Gonaives, Haiti.

Gonaives is the second largest city in Haiti, second only to Port-a-Prince. Jubilee was constructed to house a few hundred people after the floods of 2008 however it contained several thousand.

All of the residents of Jubilee lived in small home-built shanties made of anything they could find, dirt floors with no running water or sanitary facilities. The average child would never reach school age due to diseases. Mothers were making cookies from dirt and water simply to give their kids something to eat.

Everything that was planned for the week was to be done at the feeding station and school located in the heart of Jubilee. In the middle of several buildings, including the school and the feeding station there was a gazebo made of rock and palm leaves. I would sit in the gazebo to have a little shade from the scorching Haitian heat. Eventually some children, small and a little older, would come and sit with me.

We could not speak each other's language, so we started a process of "see and do." I would point at something, a mountain, a dog, or horse or building and say the name in English. They would say the name in Creole. Our mutual education began.

On our second day, I stopped at a local street market in Gonaives and purchased a dozen or so small books that translated Creole to English, German, French and Spanish. I gave each child in the gazebo a copy.

I felt like I was doing something productive, and I was also staying out of the way of the ones who came on the mission trip with an objective. On the day that we left Jubilee, most of the kids in the gazebo cried, as did I. We're now going to fast forward several years and several trips to Haiti.

One of the missionaries, an interpreter and I were invited to a one-day seminar to be held in Cap Haitian, located on the northern coast of Haiti. The seminar was mostly European types (white skin) as well as a few Haitians who were working cooperatively to bring positive change to Haiti.

The seminar was an eye-opener for me. There are a lot of people around the world who want to do good for mankind. Some of these people have dedicated their lives to this cause.

On our way back to Gonaives (a five-hour drive across the mountains) we were looking into one of the most beautiful sunsets I've ever seen, and I commented on "God's beauty in everything." During our conversation, our interpreter said to me "PaPa Boyce (a name the Haitians gave me because of my gray hair) you don't realize, do you?"

I looked at him and said, "What are you talking about?" He said, "PaPa Boyce, I was one of those boys in the gazebo that you taught English to on your first trip to Haiti." Once I realized who he was, we both sobbed like little children.

This young man told me a story about losing his book just a few short days after I left. He borrowed a book from a friend of his and copied it word for word. This young man was successful from all Haitian standards, and he was our interpreter as well as our guide.

He also owned a couple of tap-taps. A tap-tap is a makeshift taxi. You put as many people as you can on this truck and when they want to get off, they simply tap- tap on the roof, thus the name. To know that I had even such a small part in this young man's life made all the hardships of Haitian trips worth everything I had spent ten times over.

The only other Haitian story that I would like to share is during my five weeks in Port Salute (Located on the western peninsula.) One day, I was walking down the main street in Port Salute looking to buy some pates (la pate) for breakfast. A very strange man walked on the opposite side of the road from me. He would not make eye contact with me and kept his distance. He wore clothes that were way too large for him. He held his pants up with one hand and fiddled with his hair with the other.

It was obvious that he had some serious mental issues. On the second morning, while making the same trip to pick up breakfast, I encountered this man again. Once again, he crossed the road and wouldn't make eye contact with me. I spoke to him, but he acted as though he didn't hear me. I was determined to make friends with this guy.

It was obvious that he was an outcast among his own people. On the third day, I purchased an extra pate and when we met this time, I walked across the road and reached out my hand with the pate and basically shoved it in his face. He snatched it and rushed away.

I did this for several days and eventually, when he saw me, he would walk up to me with his hand out. I would always have a pate for him. It wasn't long before when he saw me coming, he would smile and walk straight up to me, and we'd smile at each other. We never talked and I have no idea of his eventual fate.

I was told by some locals that he was a "zombie." Most people aren't aware, but zombies really do exist, not as the movies depict them but in a much more sinister way.

I was told that it has been a practice in the Caribbean to kidnap young men and women and treat them to a very strong, locally grown drug to basically turn them into mindless slaves. These drugged humans have been used in factories as well as farms as cheap labor for centuries.

The man I met each morning was one of the unfortunate individuals who had escaped his owner and lived a hermit's life in the woods next to the sea. It should be noted that most, if not all, zombies in Haiti are owned by rich black Haitians. If you think that slavery is over, think again. Most Haitian law officials turn their back on such crimes due to the fear created by the folklore of the "living dead."

I always find it amazing how God puts people in need directly in the paths of those who can do just the right thing at the right time to add a little happiness to their life. I also believe in His ability to make changes in all of our lives that are eternal and lasting. I wonder what my PaPa would think if he saw "Pee-Wee" fraternizing with zombies in Haiti. Like I've said before, you simply can't make this stuff up.

This story could go on and on for many more pages and stories, but it's my desire to entertain and educate my family on my life experiences. I don't want them to become so bored that they won't read this book cover to cover.

My grandson, Keaton Patterson, and me near the island of "Ile-a-Vache" (Island of Cows), Haiti.

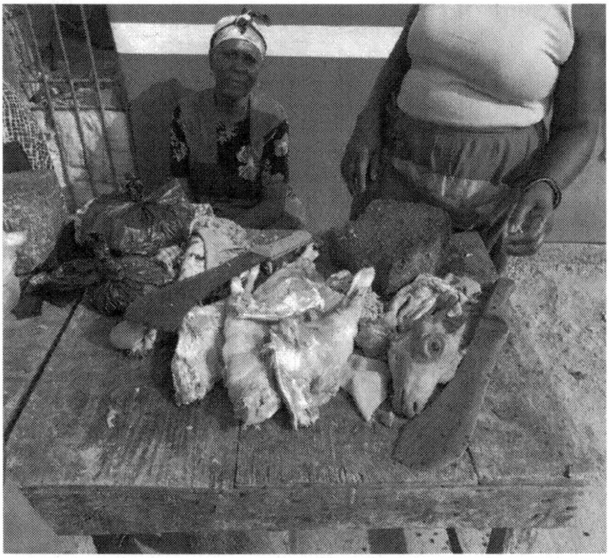

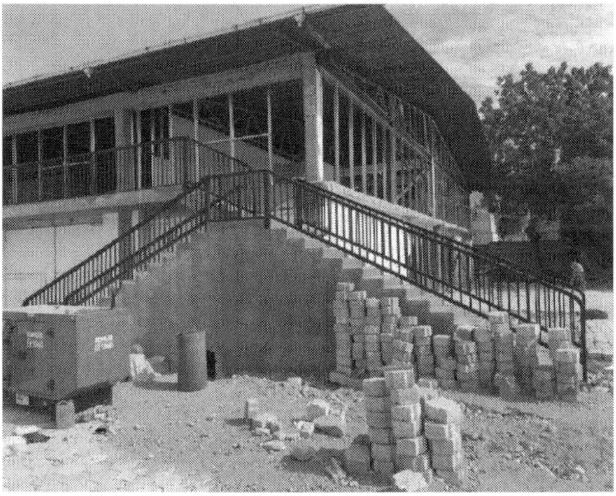

A real human skeleton on a vacant lot in Gonaives, Haiti.

It's also my desire that these life experiences can be passed on to my children, grandchildren, and great grandchildren and future descendants alike.

I want my family to know where they came from and what, by the grace of God, they can do to overcome all obstacles. Contrary to a common concept of our times, life is NOT all about us.

The fulfillment and joy we experience out of life is directly proportional to what we do for others.

This life is nothing more than a mist in the wind. It'll be over before you know it. Enjoy it to the max, and remember:

1. Try to leave each person you encounter better than when you met them.
2. Do no harm.
3. Love is God's most important commandment.
4. There can never be full enjoyment of life without forgiveness first.
5. Forgiveness rarely results in restoration of relationships, however without it your soul will never be at peace.
6. You don't have to like someone to respect them.

7. Without exception, everyone deserves respect.
8. Being a dictator never accomplishes all that you are capable of, two or more working together for the common good of the whole is much preferred.
9. Without compromise, there is no civilization.
10. Family is more important than gold.
11. Wealth is by no means everything.
12. Last, but not least, death is also a gift from God for without death, life would not be worth living.

This is my story and I'm sticking to it!

God Bless!

# RECOMMENDED READING LIST

This recommended reading list is not in any particular order of importance, not by title or author or importance to me, they are simply some of the books I've read and enjoyed.

- ❏ The Holy Bible inspired by God
- ❏ All the Light We Cannot See by Anthony Doerr
- ❏ Lost in Shangri-La by Mitchell Zuckoff
- ❏ Decision Points by George W. Bush
- ❏ The Presidents Club by Nancy Gibbs and Michael Duffy
- ❏ Miracle at Midway by Gordon W. Prange
- ❏ Triumph Forsaken (The Vietnam War, 1954-1965) by Mark Moyar
- ❏ Storming Heaven by Dale Brown
- ❏ Trail of Tears (The rise and fall of the Cherokee Nation) by John Ehle
- ❏ Killing Patton by Bill O'Reilly and Martin Dugard
- ❏ John Adams by David McCullough
- ❏ Team of Rivals by Doris Kearns Goodwin
- ❏ Behind the Lines by W.E.B. Griffin
- ❏ Red Rabbit by Tom Clancy
- ❏ A Pilot's Journey (Memoirs of a Tuskegee Airman) by Curtis Christopher Robinson
- ❏ Midnight in the Garden of Good and Evil by John Berend
- ❏ This Present Darkness by Frank E. Peretti
- ❏ Tom Sawyer and Huckleberry Finn by Mark Twain
- ❏ The Teeth of the Tiger by Tom Clancy
- ❏ Killing Jesus by Bill O'Reilly & Martin Dugard

- ❏ The Printer of Udell's (A story of the Middle West) by Harold Bell Wright
- ❏ Killing Lincoln by Bill O'Reilly & Martin Dugard
- ❏ Matterhorn (A novel of the Vietnam War) by Karl Marlantes
- ❏ A bold fresh piece of Humanity by Bill O'Reilly
- ❏ Capital Gaines by (Smart things learned doing stupid stuff) by Chip Gaines
- ❏ On Hallowed Ground (A story of Arlington National Cemetery) by Robert M. Poole
- ❏ A Better War (Unexamined victories and final tragedy of America's last year in Vietnam) by Lewis Sorley
- ❏ Flags of our Fathers by James Bradley with Ron Powers
- ❏ Flyboys by James Bradley
- ❏ Flight of the Intruder by Stephen Coonts
- ❏ Race to the Top of the World by Sheldon Bart
- ❏ The Innocent Man by John Grisham
- ❏ The Things They Carried by Tim O'Brien
- ❏ Going After Cacciato by Tim O'Brien
- ❏ Disclosure by Michael Crichton
- ❏ Deception Point by Dan Brown
- ❏ Run for Your Life by James Patterson and Michael Ledwidge
- ❏ EndWar by Tom Clancy
- ❏ Roll of Thunder, Hear My Cry by Mildred D. Taylor
- ❏ The Associate by John Grisham
- ❏ For Whom the Bell Tolls by Ernest Hemingway
- ❏ The Old Man and the Sea by Ernest Hemingway
- ❏ Farewell to Arms by Ernest Hemingway
- ❏ Dispatches from Pluto by Richard Grant

# A LIFE WORTH LIVING

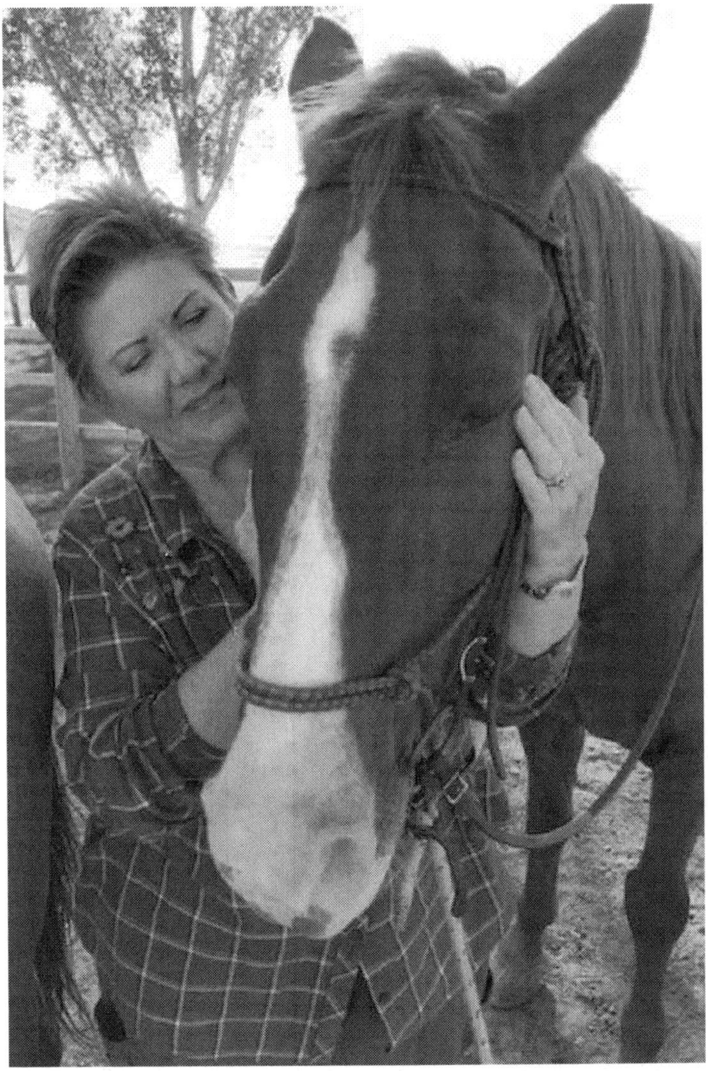

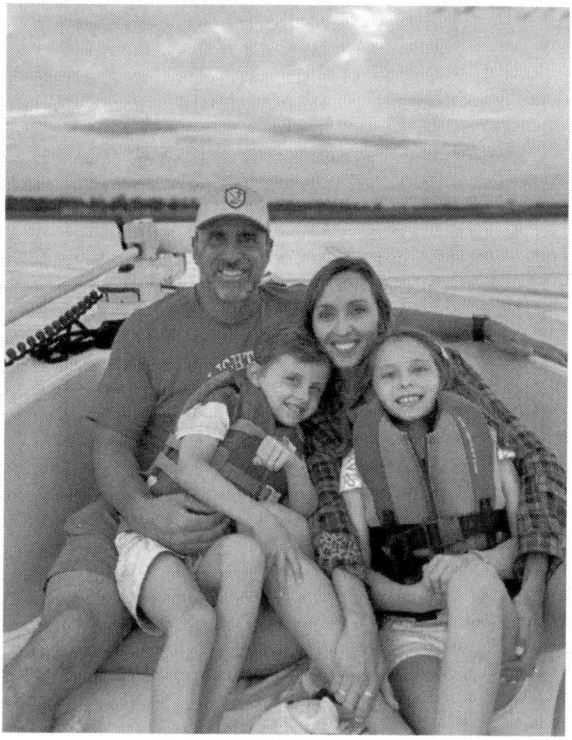

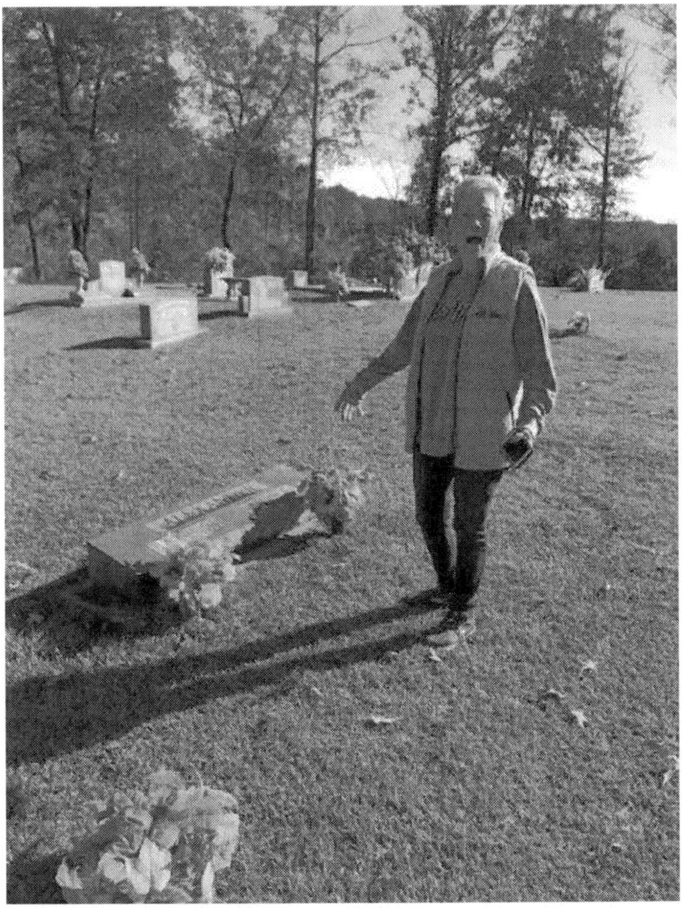

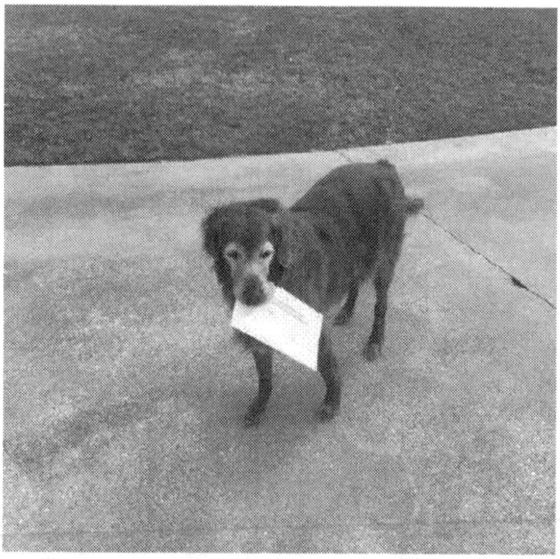

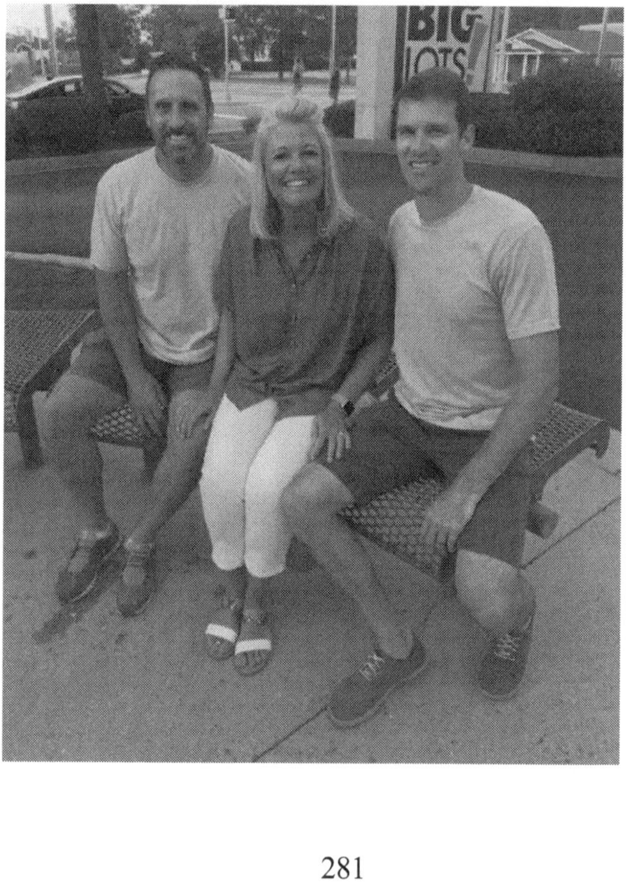
BIG

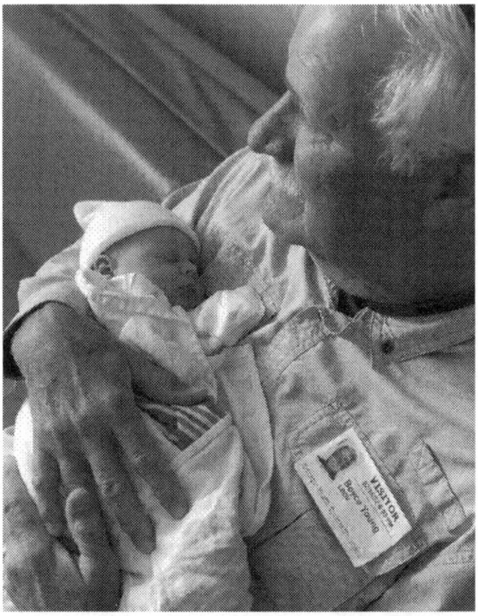
VISITOR

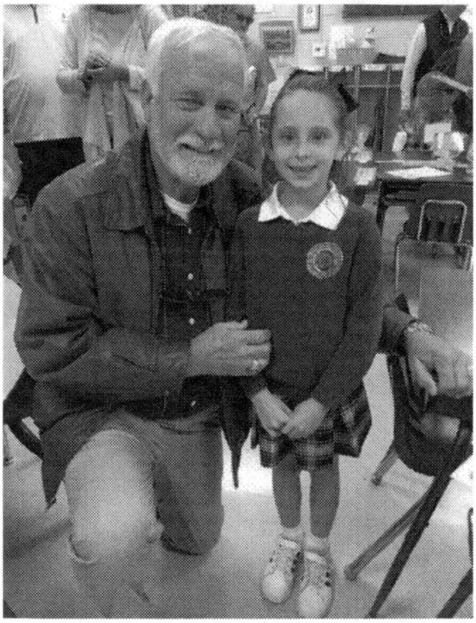

Dear friend, David Kelly

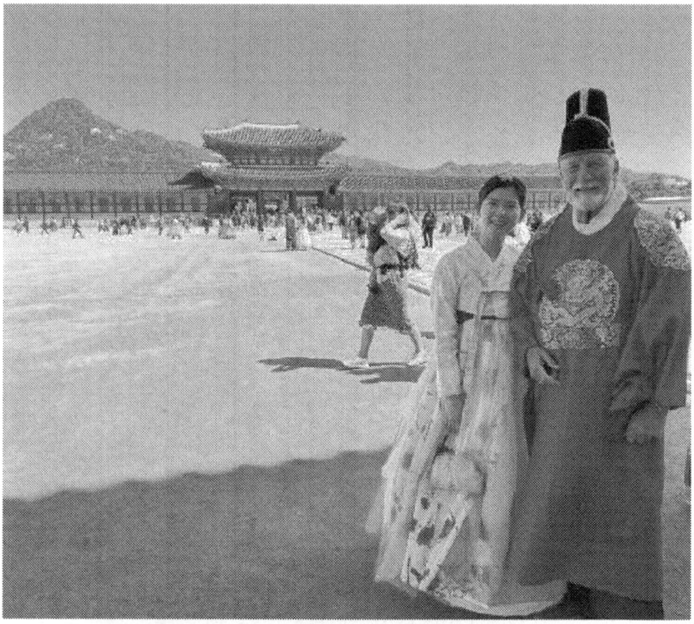

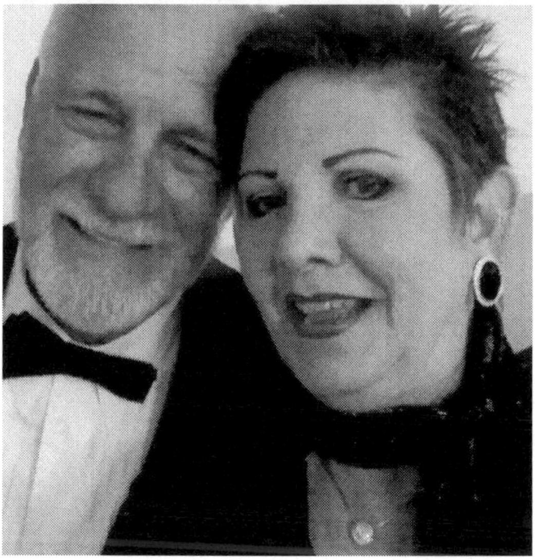

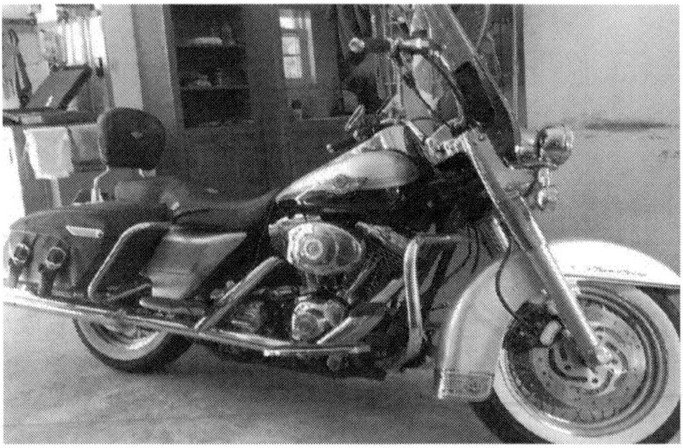

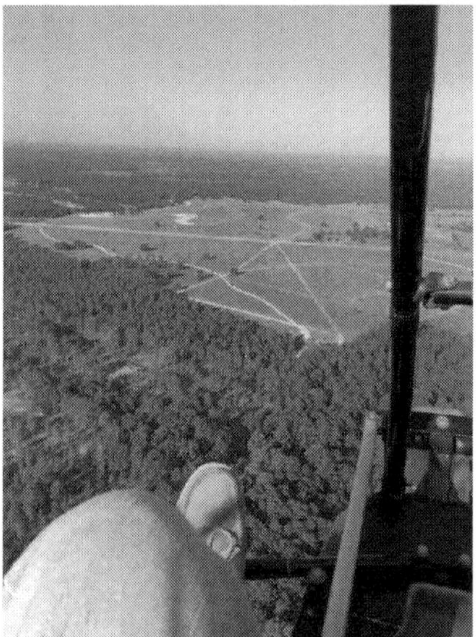

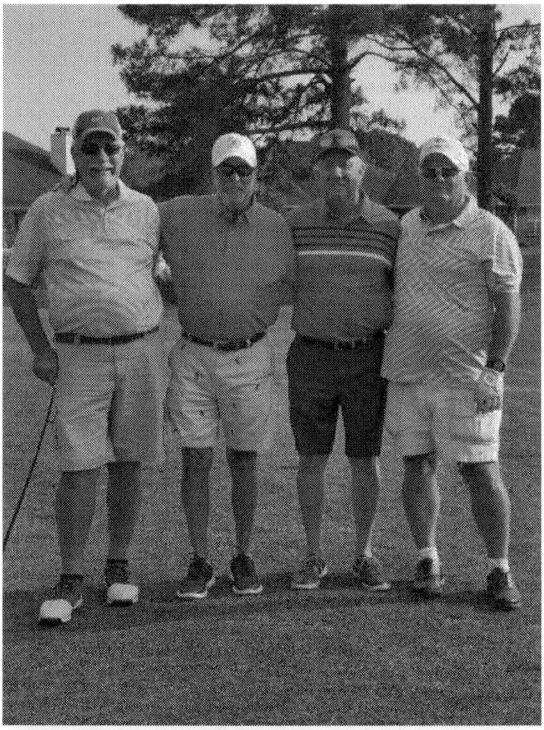

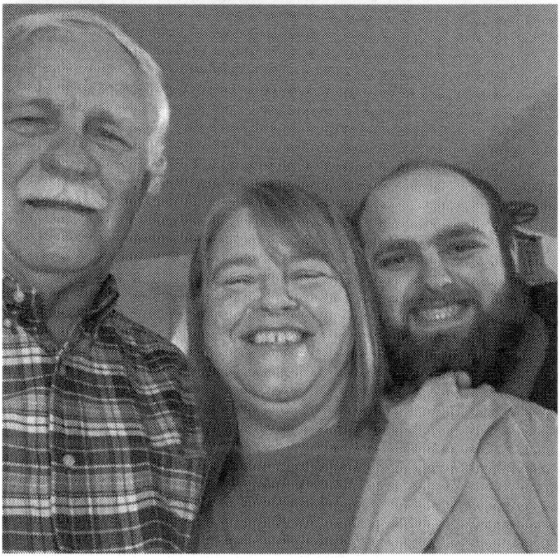

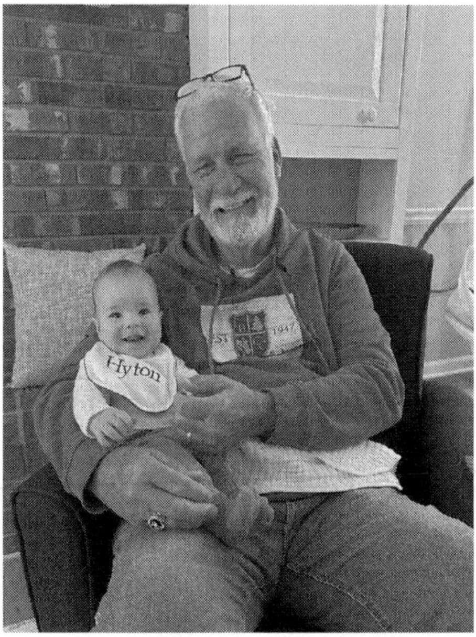
Hyton

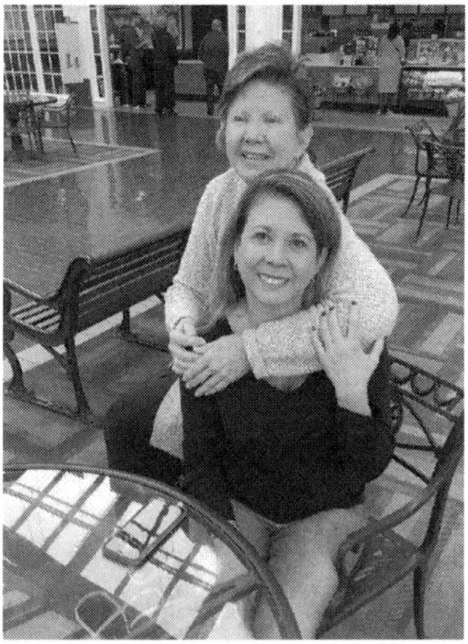

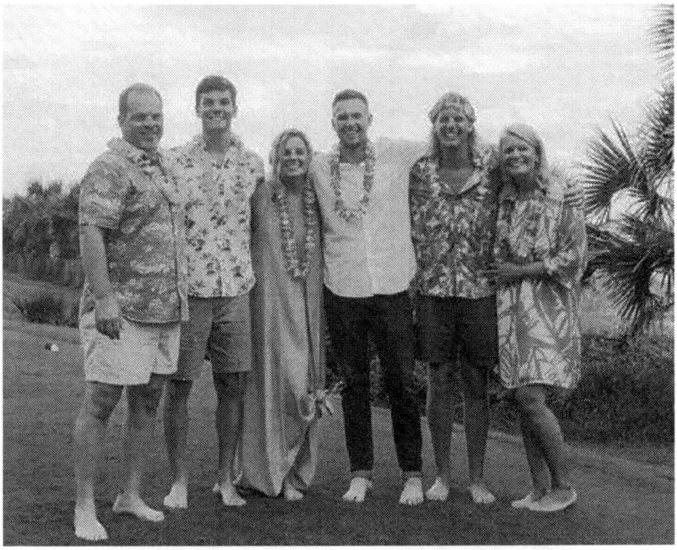

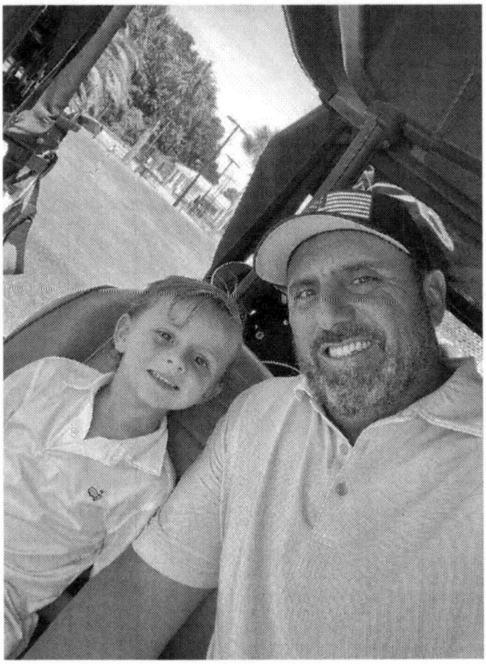

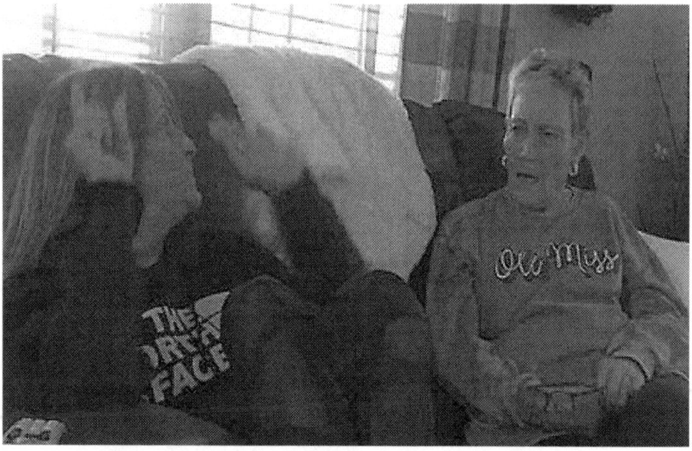
THE
FACE
Ole Miss

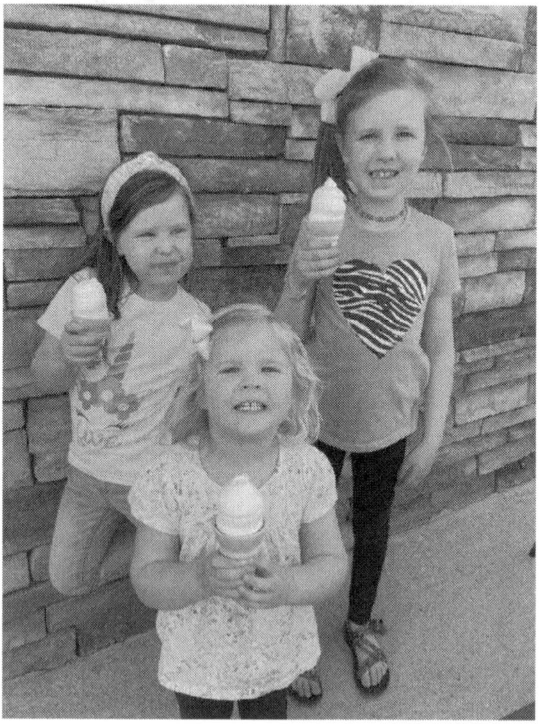

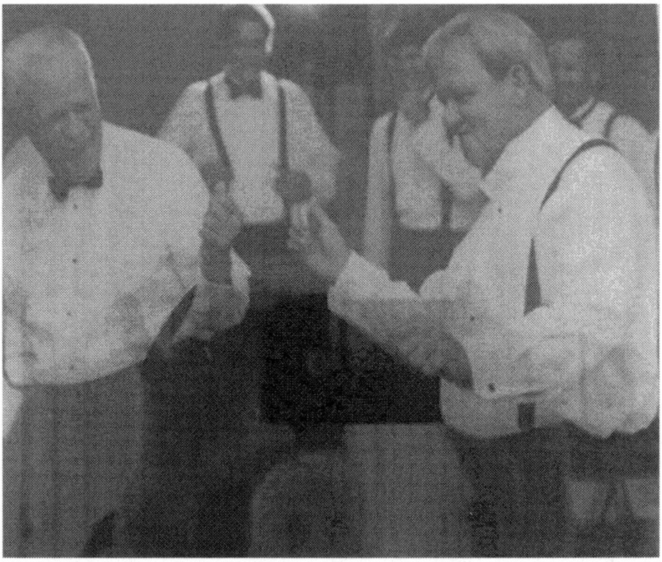

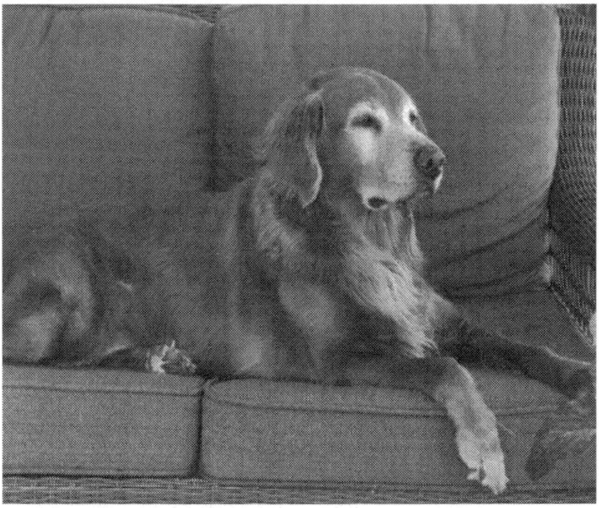

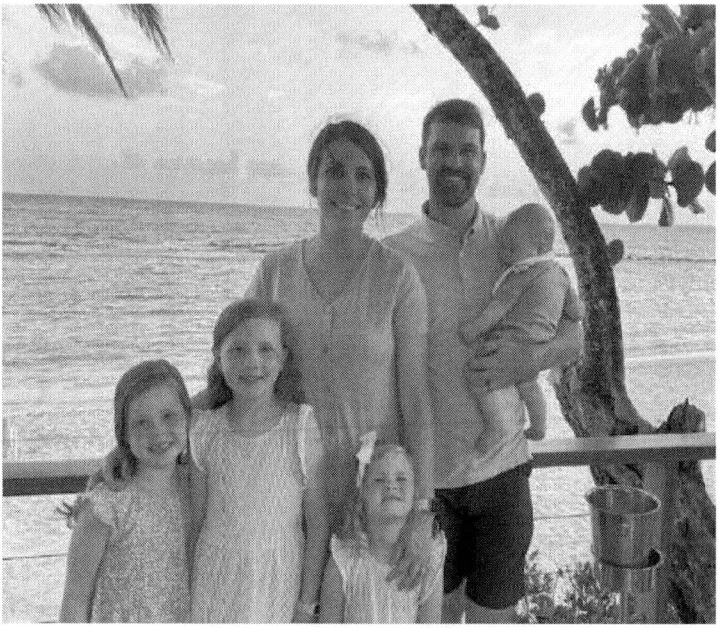

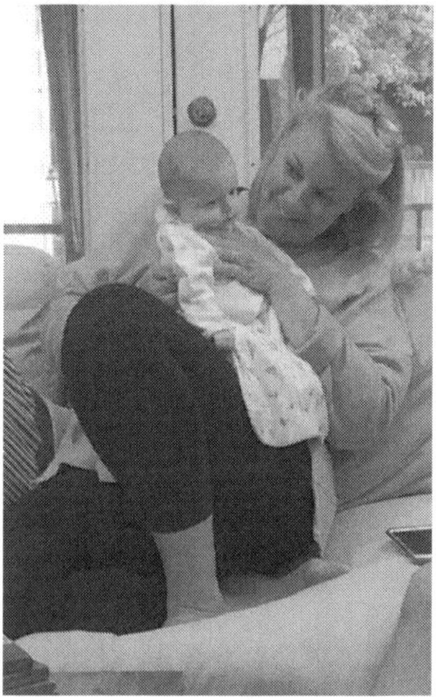

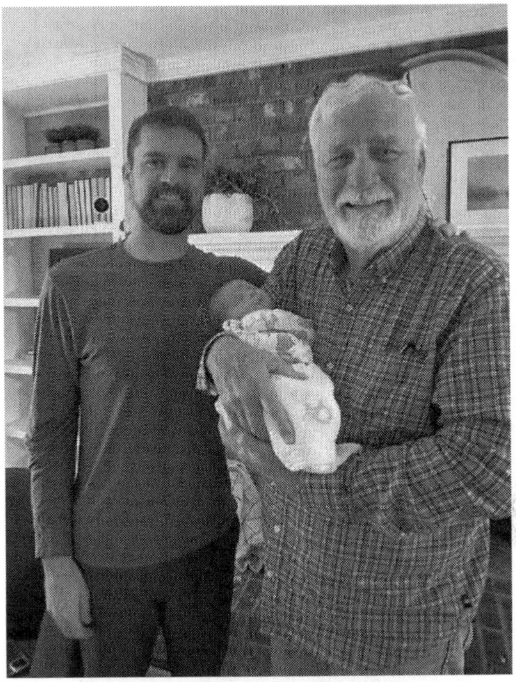

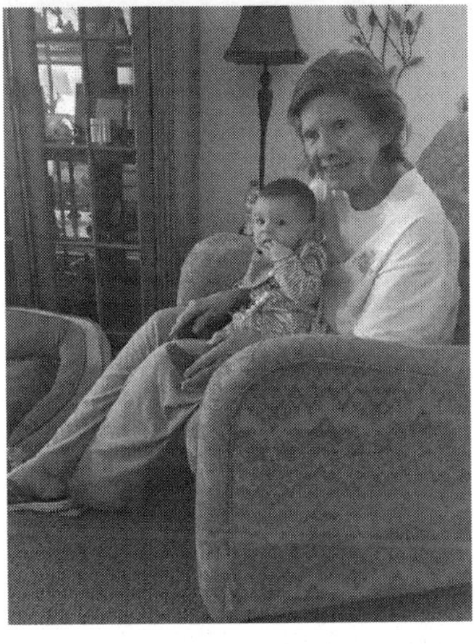

this is my new favorite photo it'll never not be my favorite photo because she's also a genius and put the remote up to her ear like this when i said "hello" she's perfect my god!!!!!

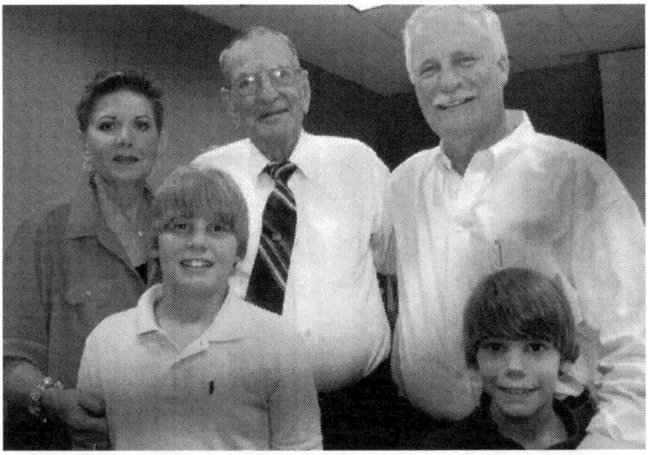

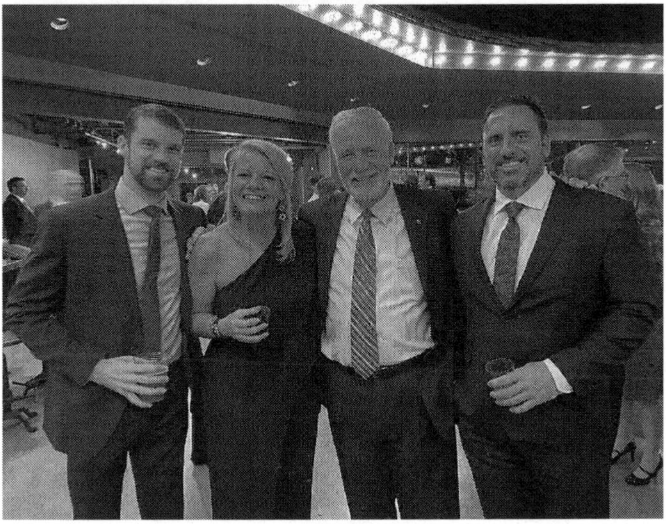

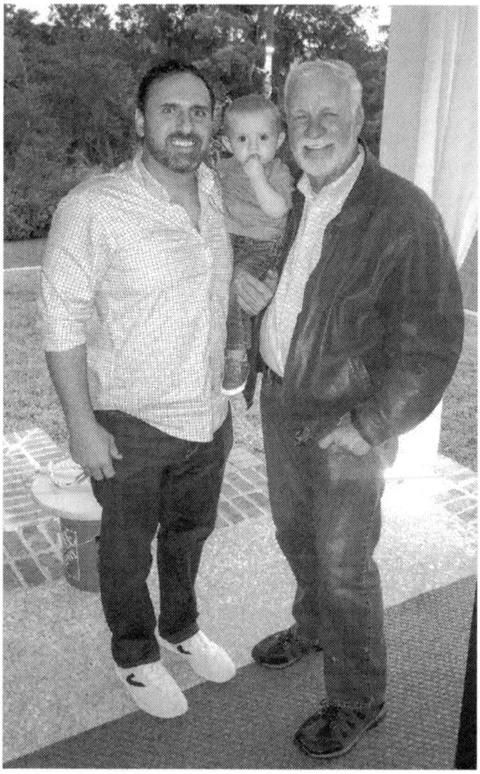

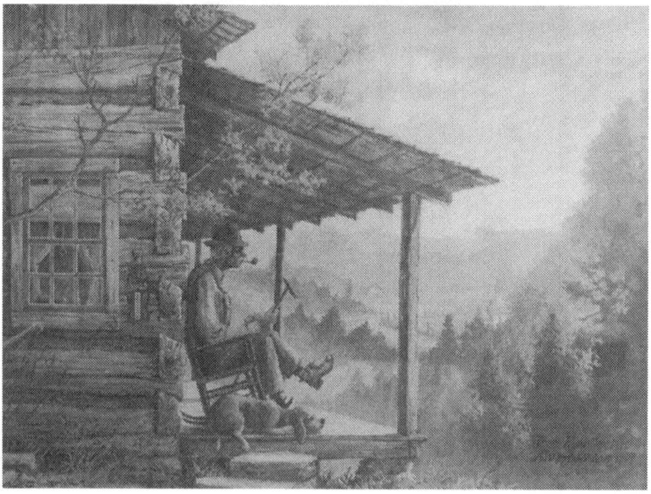

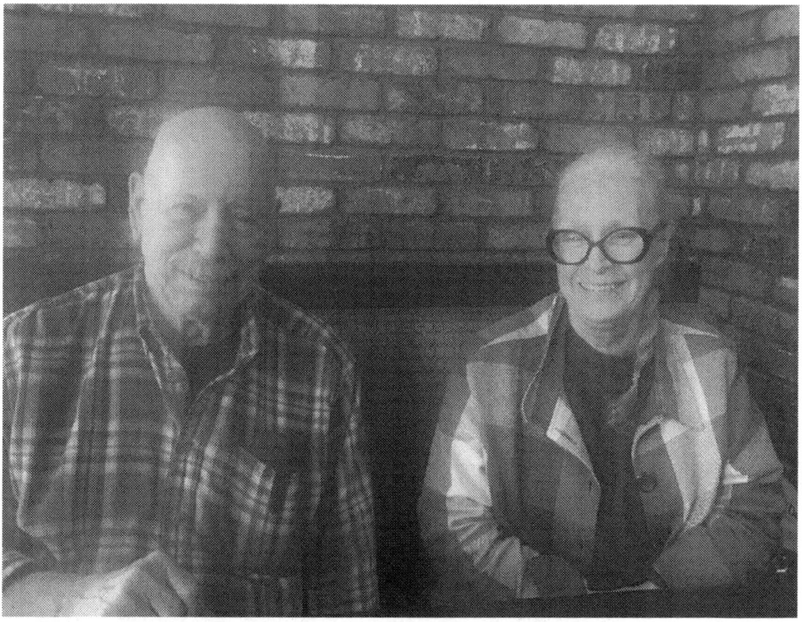

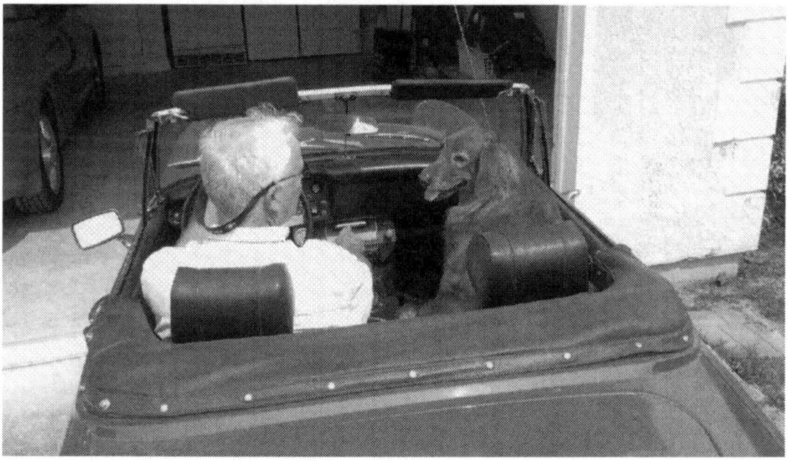

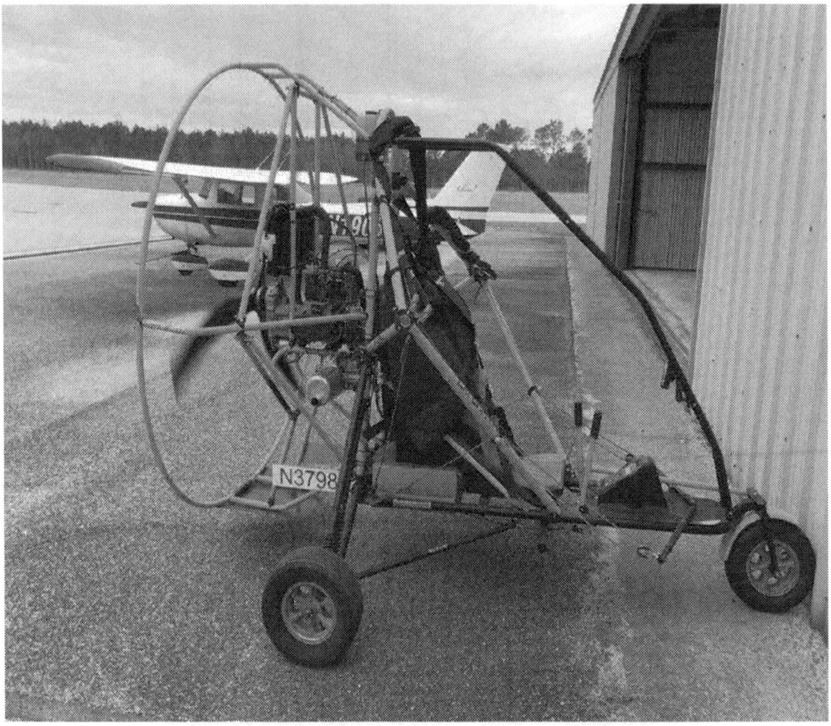
N3798

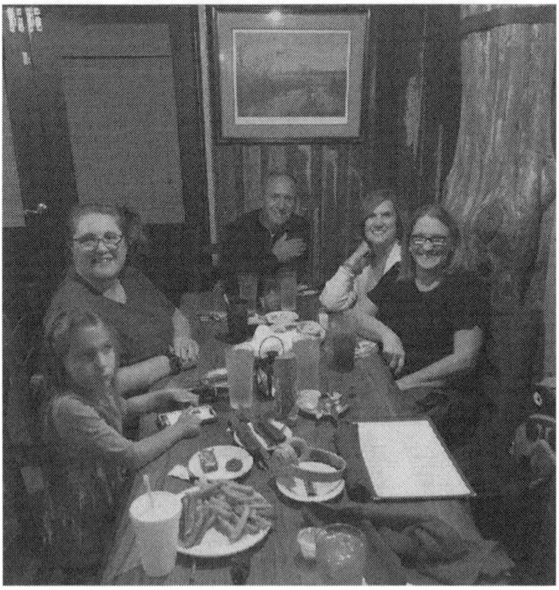

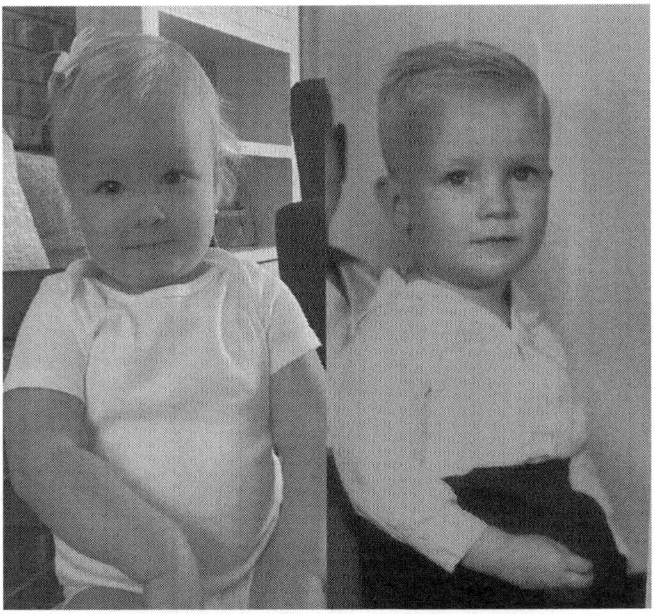

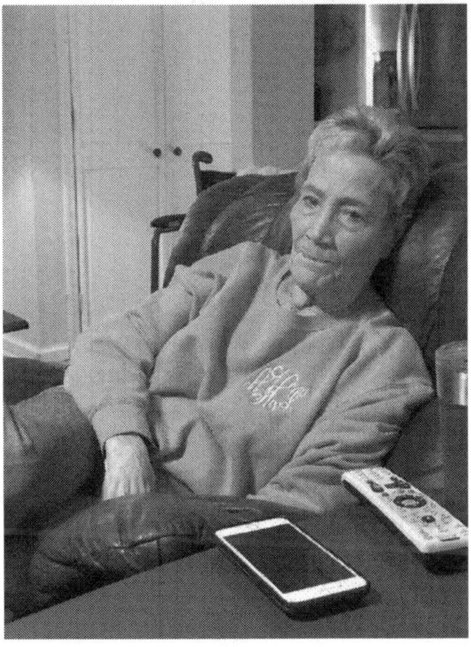

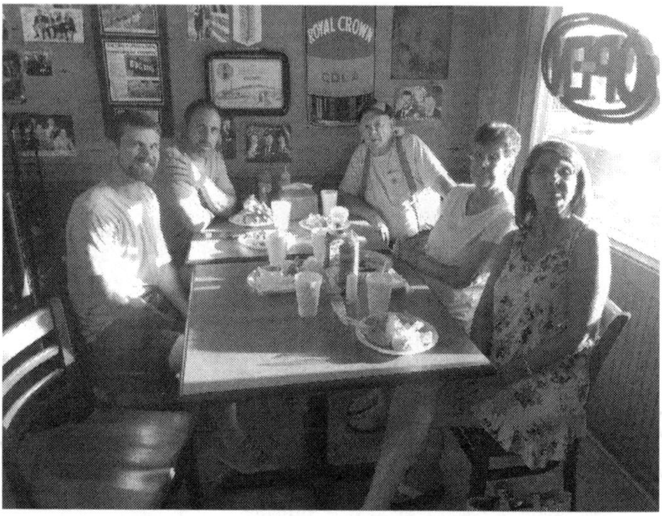
ROYAL CROWN
COLA

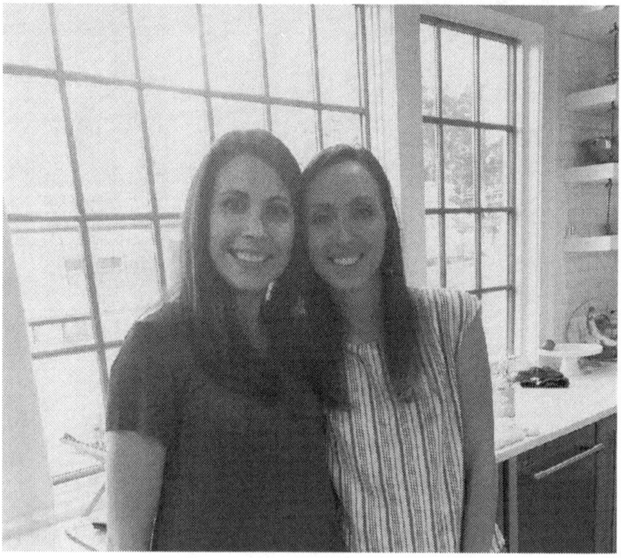

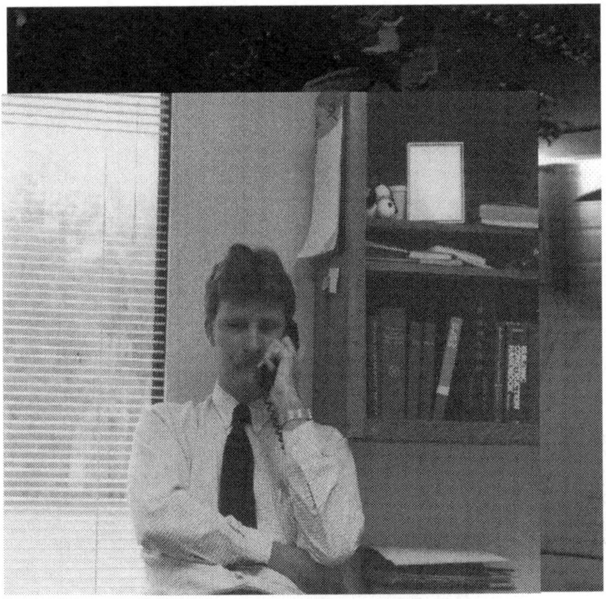

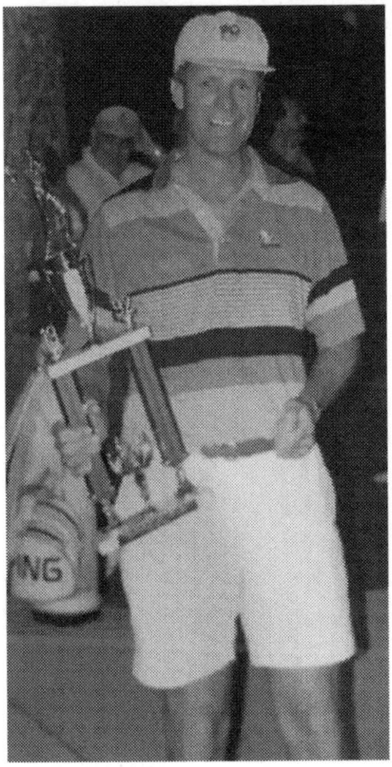

Life is worth living!
(Christmas 2023)

Made in the USA
Columbia, SC
06 August 2024